*A Year
Without Fear*

Jeremy P. Tarcher/Penguin
a member of Penguin Group (USA)
New York

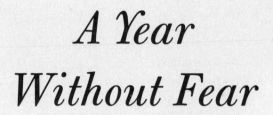

A Year Without Fear

365 DAYS OF MAGNIFICENCE

. . . .

TAMA KIEVES

JEREMY P. TARCHER/PENGUIN
Published by the Penguin Group
Penguin Group (USA) LLC
375 Hudson Street
New York, New York 10014

USA · Canada · UK · Ireland · Australia
New Zealand · India · South Africa · China

penguin.com
A Penguin Random House Company

Most Tarcher/Penguin books are available at special quantity discounts for bulk
purchase for sales promotions, premiums, fund-raising, and educational needs.
Special books or book excerpts also can be created to fit specific needs. For
details, write: Special.Markets@us.penguingroup.com.

Library of Congress Cataloging-in-Publication Data

Kieves, Tama J.
A year without fear : 365 days of magnificence / Tama Kieves.
    p.   cm.
ISBN 978-0-399-17353-0
1. Fear. I. Title.
BF575.F2K54   2015   2014035245
152.4'6—dc23

Printed in the United States of America
5 7 9 10 8 6 4

Book design by Lauren Kolm

This is the year I stop pressing my nose up against the glass, wishing for another life.

This is the year I love with banshee strength.

This is the year I end the race. I enter the haven of a life that has waited for me all along.

This is the year I become a master of where I place my attention. My focus is my life.

This is the year I open to the flow that will take me all the way, but not a way I know.

This is the year I'm more interested in making my wildest joys *real* rather than "realistic."

This is the year I step into greatness even while facing rejection.

This is the year I wake up to the story of a lifetime, because I have become a storyteller who knows Great Love.

This is a year without fear.

Introduction

. . . .

What you think you are is a belief to be undone.

—*A Course in Miracles*

What Would Your Life Be Like—If You Had No Fear?

I'd love you to step beyond the hypnotism of what you think you can and cannot do. Here's what's true:

You are loved.
You have everything you need.
You are more powerful than you know.

But fear or unquestioned negative beliefs, old stories, the voices of the media, or maybe those around you, may keep you from your boldest possibilities. Well, that's about to change.

I doubt you want a "mediocre" life. I doubt you want to just pay your bills or settle for a *sort of* loving relationship and call it good. I think you want to cry with gratitude when it's all said and done. I'd like you to cry before then.

This is your life. This is your chance. This is your time on earth.

I want you to write the screenplay that moans in your bloodstream. I want you to love your child like no child has ever been loved before. I want you to run for office or run from your office or whatever nudges you in the sanctum of your heart. I want you to know the peace of the Dalai Lama, more freeing than a nice big bucket of Xanax, and a mainline of gratitude sweeter than any Starbucks Frappuccino.

And I want you to laugh so freely your stomach hurts, just like you did when you were a kid. I want you to forgive yourself. I want you to fall madly in love with your husband or meet the love of your life and go skinny-dipping in the olive-green lake of your childhood.

I want you to leave behind the situation that squats on your spirit like a sumo wrestler. I want you to eat better, drink less, or whatever nourishes and respects your precious body. I want you to take that vacation in Italy, take your company public, or sprawl out in your own backyard paradise in Poughkeepsie, drinking lemonade and watching blue jays on a Thursday. I want you to hit the note you came to sing— because life is set up for you to do that. I want you to know the Presence of a strength not of this world.

I want you to drop your predictable goals and drop your jaw in awe—as you discover what you can *really* have this year.

Forget about striving for only what you think you can have. I want to coach you into the extraordinary life that's calling to you now.

Through five-minute mind-set shifts, I want to help you uncover your astonishing potential, your own authentic steps or shifts, and the uncanny progress that develops from a radically loving relationship with yourself, others, and your life. *The inspired power within you can accomplish anything at any time.* Let this be your time.

Welcome to a year without fear.

Why I Wrote This Daily Guide

Years ago as an overworked and soul-starved attorney, I walked along a beach and breathed in salt-drenched air, feeling as though I might want to end my life. Instead, I made the decision to begin my life in earnest. I made the wild and unorthodox decision to let go of that career, to let go of what society told me was safe and beneficial. I realized that it was fear that had compelled me to play it "safe," attend Harvard Law School, graduate with honors, and work a bazillion hours for a major law firm—even though I had always dreamed of being a writer, not a lawyer.

But I hadn't called my motivation fear. I called it "being realistic." I was just "being practical," living life the way I'd been told you should live it.

It was only when I stopped making choices out of fear that I discovered a whole new way to live. I had to learn to trust in a power beyond my intellect and a love that was more powerful than any resource I'd ever known. I had to learn how to love myself through bouts of anxiety and frustration into creativity, conviction, and inspired action. I began teaching and coaching, and published my first book, *This Time I Dance! Creating the Work You Love,* which gradually drew a following from around the world. I followed that book with my national best seller *Inspired & Unstoppable: Wildly Succeeding in Your Life's Work!* Now I'm taking some of the wisdom from both those books as well as my e-book *A Course in Miracles for Life Ninjas* and including it here, along with other strategies and approaches I've taught for years.

For the past two decades, I have been a career catalyst and inspired success coach. I've been in the media and led workshops, keynoted, and offered retreats throughout the United States and abroad. I've worked with thousands of individuals who, like me, knew they were here for *something more.* Yet they held themselves back. Many didn't even realize the depths to which they held themselves back. They just lived the life they assumed they could have.

I've seen how our own self-talk and beliefs about reality can corrode our potential. As a coach, I've seen how asking someone the right question can open up a whole new destiny. I know that real happiness or freedom doesn't come from taking the "right steps." It comes from cultivating our own inspired mind-set, the intimate, interior world we live in every single day.

Your original instincts and genius are a love song between you and God (or the Universe, Spirit, Instinctive Self, or whatever you call an extraordinary consciousness). You are a life that has never been here before.

When you really want to go beyond fear, it is not about force, platitudes, or manufactured behavior. That kind of impatience just leads to masking pain. True freedom is a conscious, everyday spiritual adventure. It's a reinvention. It's a wholly new relationship with yourself.

I know you can achieve any inspired goal in your own inspired way. I want to see you thrive. I know it all depends on you generating a miraculous mind-set through daily choices. Are you choosing from fear or love? Insecurity or strength? Conditioning or intentionality? Are you letting go of self-criticism and becoming fiercely supportive of yourself and others?

You're making decisions every single day and, really, innumerable times during the day. I want to help you constantly make the ones that inspire your greatest love.

There is a way to live a fearless life.

And it's a magnificent practice—a practice in flourishing for the rest of our lives.

Daily Miracles

For many, it's not "convenient" to fit radical transformation into busy calendars. So I wanted to make this work accessible. Since you may never take a weekend retreat with me or hire me as your personal coach, I wanted to come to you.

I want to fit into your backpack, your briefcase, your life, your morning ritual, or wherever I can meet you for a pow-wow. I want to remind you that you are safe. You are seeded with an invincible intrinsic wisdom. There is nothing limiting your true desires, except your limiting thoughts. I want to whisper the truth to you again and again. I want to beam so much love at you, your barriers just disintegrate into stardust. I want to encourage you to be braver than you think you can be—because you have the ability to be inspired at any second and to tap the strength of a thousand rivers converging.

I want to be the voice you're not hearing on the news or in your office—or, maybe, even in your home. Because I know you have an amazing life to live—stemming from an amazing mind-set—and it's all a matter of practice.

(By the way, if you'd like to experience these daily lessons in *audio* through your in-box [with 5-minute guided meditations to enrich and fuel your day], I'd love to offer you a week of this support for free. You can get it here: TamaKieves.com/

free365.) And please come visit my world at TamaKieves.com to discover more support and resources, and a tribe of smart, fun, creative, and conscious people just like you.

How to Use This Book

These are five-minute mind-set shifts/focuses/meditations designed to train your mind to walk into a new day. The intention you have for your day will create your day—your days create your life.

A conscious mind-set requires practice. Unfortunately, you've heard negative messages more than once. That's why reading a book and putting it down doesn't often work. *A Year Without Fear* is a possibility you feed yourself every single day.

I believe in the physics of synchronicity. I trust in your internal guidance system. I know each one of these messages will land where it needs to land. These words are vitamins, meant to feed your chemistry consistently. The truth is meant to be cumulative, repetitive, and symphonic.

These mind-set shifts are call and response. I say these words to you and your spirit answers. Your soul supplies the context, fills in the memories, or reprograms the circuits. Maybe you will try something new in your day. Your experiment will open you up to a different experience. These experiences promote your confidence. And confidence attracts exciting opportunities. You'll notice that the tiniest effort can liberate the floodgates of joy.

Here's What I Want You to Do

First, and always, I want you to do what *you* want to do. (This is a book about letting go of fear and trusting where you feel led. To me that's more important than anything, including you using this book. You're here to follow your inspired guidance, not mine.)

Each day, imagine that these words were chosen on this very day just for you, by me, your very own career/inspired success coach. Or maybe it helps you to think of these words as coming to you from a future self, the one who is living your dreams, or from the voice of your beloved Inner Teacher. Allow the message to marinate, infiltrate, speak to the electric one within you . . . and remind him or her to come out and play. You don't have to understand it or even think it applies to you.

Perhaps keep a special journal by your side. Journal any insight, commitment, or actions that come to you as you take these words in. Remember, you are entering inspired time as you read these daily invitations. The ideas, questions, or emotions that arise for you during this time are even more important than the words I wrote on the page. Pay attention to what comes up for you when you read them, as well as what arises throughout the day.

Here are some suggestions for how to use this book:

- Have a heartfelt conversation about these words with your loved one. (A breakfast ritual. Intention partner. Work team. Support group. Spirit.)
- Journal about *whatever* comes up as you meet these thoughts. Or do a yoga pose with them.
- Create an art journal around these words. Doodle, draw, paint, collage.
- Play "guidance roulette": open a page spontaneously. See what message arrives for you.

Oh, and please stay true to yourself. If you miss a day or month, don't decide that you can't still have results. Choose again. Begin to listen to your wisdom now. It's always the right time. You're never behind. Wherever you are, love will meet you there.

Daily, I will weave in a question or intention. I'm not talking to your everyday mind. I'm talking to the unlimited one within you. I'm planting suggestions and seeds of creativity. I'm reminding you of what you already know. I want this to be a daily conversation with your True Self.

Some of these daily thoughts may seem to contradict one another. For example, I might tell you to trust inaction, while another day I suggest you take an action whether you feel like it or not. Real love is a prism. And I am offering only a facet a day. Only you can decide when a truth applies to you and when it does not. And, sometimes, finding a suggestion that isn't right for you catapults you into the clarity of what is.

How Do You Get over Fear?

How do you get past that immediate impulse to fight, flee, or eat massive amounts of pasta? Let's face it—these stellar options are brought to you by the amygdala, the primitive reptilian brain that didn't know a thing about finding yourself, raising enlightened children, or getting a book deal. I don't know about you, but I don't want a lizard being in charge of my evolution and life. I want an eagle. I want an angel. I want to choose from the golden throne of being centered, alive, and attuned to what I really want. That's what I want for you, too. You will make exponentially different choices from a different part of yourself.

When I was in therapy, I just wanted to cut the fear out—do a lobotomy—or burn it to a pulp. But it turns out (no matter how much you offer to pay these people) that you do not remove fear by attacking it. You cannot "get rid of" fear by focusing on fear.

You let go of fear by focusing on love. Love is the answer to fear.

By love, I don't mean romantic love or pious, saccharine kindness. Love is attention, creativity, generosity, support, and the letting go of self-judgment. There are infinite ways to love and free yourself of fear.

Psychology, peak performance, religion, and spirituality all offer techniques and belief systems for how to face or overcome fear. In my own personal growth and in my work with clients and students, I'll use anything and everything that works. That said, I have taught *A Course in Miracles* (an internationally popular spiritual psychotherapy program) for twenty-five years, so of course that material runs rampant in my bloodstream. Drawing from all my studies and hands-on experience, I've tended to land on three main tenets. I offer them here, since I deliberately repeat and expand on these themes throughout this book:

1. *Everything is either love or fear.* The best way to get out of fear is to get into love. If you focus on something you love or you do something you love or you hold love for another, your fear will not be there. You cannot feel fear in the same moment that you are feeling love.

2. *Stay in the present moment.* All fear comes from thinking about the future or thinking about the past. In the present moment, absent self-judgment, all is well. You connect with your own wholeness and true light.

3. *There is another way to see everything.* If you are in fear, you are seeing something from a painful point of view. You are telling a painful story. There is another way to experience this. There is a loving perspective that will free you. When you are connected to your Spirit, there are no remaining painful stories.

For most of us, moving beyond fear is not an overnight shift. It's not a pill. It's a practice. It's a pilgrimage. It's a commitment to fill our minds with new conditioning, new perspectives— basically, the ideals that set us free.

By the way, fear, as I'm talking about it, isn't just terror. It's insecurity. Shame. Anger. Bitterness. Guilt. Frustration. Anything that blocks your peace of mind or joy. Or holds you back from what you desire. People ask me, "You mean I shouldn't ever have fear? What about normal fear like when I see a tiger?"

I am all for your natural and brilliant instincts. I bless the fight-or-flight response that saves your life. I do not bless the kind of fear that destroys or drains your life. There is a difference. Likewise, I bless the healing face of grief or the kind of anger that moves you toward actions or awareness that serve your wholeness. I do not bless the emotional states that keep you stuck.

And so, dear one, let's begin. I want you to choose who

you will be in this lifetime rather than having circumstances choose for you. I want you to wake up to your own fearless potential and that of every human being. And I want you to know I'm here, believing in you, practicing in my own life, and championing the power of all our fearless love.

A Year
Without Fear

01 *january*

. . . .

As you begin this New Year, know that you are moving into a time like no other. There are wild, abundant forces gathering around you. Some of your visions have taken root and will now blossom. Some pain will evaporate. Love you can't imagine is on its way. All along, you've been preparing for this time.

Today, I practice knowing that I am moving into a time like no other.

02 *january*

. . . .

You're in this life to love. You're here to go
all in. Sure, you might get rejected by a job,
gatekeeper, or lover. *But the love that comes
through you comes to you.* You expand by
sharing your soul. In this New Year,
shrinking is over. It's time to give this life
everything you've got.

*Today, I know that in this New Year,
shrinking is over. I am here to go all in.*

03 *january*

. . . .

Astonish yourself in this lifetime. Discover
your own faculties. You did not come here to
settle on the sidelines and watch others live
their dreams. When did you stop believing
you could have what *you* wanted? Why did
you stop believing? Burn this story. Begin
again. You are anointed. You are not alone.
Give the Universe another chance to give you
your chance.

*Today, I begin again. I am willing to
give myself another chance to have what
I want.*

04 *january*

. . . .

When you're in transition, you are in the boot
camp of mysterious powers. You leave behind
the protection and the hindrance of the familiar.
Sometimes you are stripped of worldly
comforts, casual identities, and chances to
just coast. These times may bring you to your
knees. Sometimes it's only limits that can
teach us how unlimited we are.

*Today, I realize that it is my current
"limits" that will teach me how
unlimited I am.*

05 *january*

. . . .

When you do what you came here to do,
it makes you stronger. When you do not do
what you came here to do, it makes you
weaker. Sometimes, in a weak place, you feel
you have no energy, ability, or self-confidence
to act. You may feel just a bit more like a
jellyfish with a tide going the wrong way than,
say, the tiger you'd hoped you'd be. But you're
wrong. When you move toward your light,
your feet find solid ground. It's not you who
empowers your gifts. Your gifts empower you.

Today, I take any small step toward
doing or discovering what I came
here to do.

06 *january*

. . . .

Feeling fear doesn't mean things aren't
working out. Sometimes, the bigger your
dreams, the louder your fears. This is a path
of learning how to be gentle with yourself,
and also fierce. Just because a part of you
believes you are never going to have what you
desire doesn't make it true. The real truth
about you is the life beyond your fears.

Today, I know things are working out.

07 *january*

· · · · · · · · · · · · · · · · ·

It's not being "realistic" to doom yourself to stagnation. Why would you tell yourself that you could achieve only that which you've already experienced? You're still developing, aren't you? It's never realistic to deny the miraculous. That's annihilation. The reality is—you are a miracle. You are a growing, conscious vessel of the infinite and alive. Your inner voice is the compass between the landscapes of what you currently know and what you may yet know in your lifetime.

Today, I remember that I am more than what I've experienced. I am a growing, conscious expression of infinite love.

08 *january*

. . . .

Do you feel like your true expression will cost you the approval of others? It might. But it will attract the people you really want. Your wild truth will awaken the creativity and resourcefulness of other people, people you don't even know yet, people you may not even know you want to know—people who can get things done. *You will have your people.* (From *Inspired & Unstoppable: Wildly Succeeding in Your Life's Work!*)

Today, I will trust that my true expression will call my right people to me.

. . . .

Inspiration is an invitation to new abundance. It's not just the invitation to create a song, a business, a soufflé, or a screenplay. It's the invitation to create yourself. The creator is changed by the created. Yet if you refuse to listen to your own new ideas, you hold back the unlimited within you. You may think you're just being "reasonable." But how could it ever be rational to deny your greatest powers?

Today, I pay attention to my new ideas.

10 *january*

· · · · · · · · · · · · · · · · ·

Today, don't just go to your desk or kitchen.
Make the familiar your "temple," the place
where you are made anew. Everyone you meet
is secretly asking you to hold their hand, ease
their fears, and accept them. We're all in this
together. Today, be a lover, a mystic, and a
presence. Pierce the veil. Extend compassion.

*Today, I will be a lover, a mystic, and
the presence of compassion.*

11 *january*

. . . .

It is not "selfish" to pursue your interests,
respond to what brings you joy, and turn your
life into one lotus flower opening in sunlight.
It's responsible. You are responsible to the
calling within you. When you do things you
love to do, you become free of inner anguish.
You radiate generosity. You have light to give
the world.

*Today, I act responsibly by doing
something I love.*

12 *january*

In yoga, the slower you move, the stronger you become. It's true of major transitions, too. If you don't rush into things, you build heat and an inner relationship with yourself that can move through anything. The point of transition isn't to get somewhere else. It's to become someone else.

Today, I am willing to go slower in my life and build heat and a relationship with myself.

13 *january*

. . . .

You cannot listen to self-judgment and your
Inspired Self at the same time. Self-judgment
doesn't make you stronger. It makes your
fear stronger. Let go of self-judgment—by
realizing it is never telling you the truth—
and clarity and joy will emerge. Take the
nurturing road. It's the only way to inspired
power.

*Today, I remember that when I'm
listening to self-judgment, I cannot
hear the voice of Guidance.*

14 *january*

. . . .

Thinking "positively" doesn't mean your car
insurance company doesn't double your rates at the
exact moment you lose your job and also discover
you need a new part for your car, say, an *engine*. It
doesn't mean your loved one doesn't eat fourteen
scones and a gallon of cookie dough ice cream
before taking his insulin shot so as to control his
diabetes. It doesn't mean you get the contract. *It
does mean you continue to show up for life with love.*
You remain present and take continuous, empowered
actions no matter what. This transforms the quality
of your every experience. Now you're not hoping for
results. You're already getting them.

*Today, I show up with love no matter
what.*

15 *january*

. . . .

The old ways are falling apart. Some call it an
evolution of consciousness. We are the ones
who are discovering our sacred resources and
responses and bringing them to the table.
We are the ones who launch new enterprises,
discover new ways to feed more people, fight
for justice, or sing praises to the divine, even
as the stock market rumbles or the media
sings a litany of warnings. We do not ignore
reality, nor do we limit ourselves to the dim
projections of fear. We are learning how to
recognize and utilize the magnificence within
that is never threatened or taken away.

*Today, I open to the magnificence
within me that empowers me with
startling new resources.*

16 *january*

. . . .

There is nothing accidental in your life.
Perfection is not optional or variable. The
Universe is loving, intelligent, vibrational,
and working on every level and you are its
number-one priority, as is everyone else.
You can't get this wrong. You can make
yourself feel wrong. But you can't get this
wrong. Your higher nature has your highest
good in order.

Today, I know that no matter what
happens, I can't get this wrong.

17 *january*

. . . .

Crave answers? I've seen people slap and patch together decisions just so they could leave the wilderness of not knowing. Hungry for certainty, they sign up for programs, go back to school, take the job that's offered, rather than stay honest with themselves. These forced answers will come apart with the first strong wind. I'd suggest letting go of the need to figure out what you will do with the rest of your life.

What do you know just for this instant? Each moment is a bread crumb that will lead you to the gingerbread house.

Today, I focus on the bread crumbs.

18 *january*

· · · · · · · · · · · · · · · · ·

Sometimes practicality is so impractical.
A part of you may think it's wise to tone
down the intensity of what you really want,
and just go for what you think you can have.
But if you want to go the distance, go with
truth. Admit your "wild want." Because if
you compromise your desire, you will
compromise your strength.

Today, I admit my "wild want."

19 *january*

. . . .

You do not make your decisions based on facts.
You make them based on stories. The narrator
changes the story. The goddess Athena would tell
a different story than, say, the Cowardly Lion
or your thirteen-year-old self, insecure as hell.
Are you seeing your circumstance through the
narration of fear or self-criticism? Or are you
seeing "the facts" through the eyes of fierce
self-love? Your perspective will change the
nature of what you see, what you do, and what
you create in your life.

Today, I look at the facts through the
eyes of brave self-love. How would the
hero within me see these circumstances?

20 *january*

. . . .

When I feel empty or isolated, I commit to
show up for myself. I sit before the dry desert.
This is an act of honor. I arrive for myself in
all conditions. I am not a festive attendant—
only interested in my own company when
I am light and crackling with mental clarity
like lightning. My mind may be an unclear
lake right now, despite what Platitude Girl
says is on top of the hill. Showing up like
this is a practice.

*Today, I show up for myself through all
conditions.*

21 *january*

No one has more power than you. No one has
a life that is better than yours, even if they
have five houses and, it pains me to say, a
husband who really listens when they talk.
It's a grand distraction to compare. Your life
is the only adventure of its kind. Take the
time to savor the details of what feels good
to you in your life right now. Behold how
much you've grown and how much you are
growing still, and maybe even, how much
those you love have grown as well. When you
see the good that you have, you will have so
much more.

*Today, I remember that when I see the
good that I have, I will have so much
more.*

22 *january*

. . . .

It's time to stop judging other people.
You are magnificent and I don't want you
compromising your light. You judge others
only when you believe that you are limited in
some way. Perhaps you have forgotten that
you are precious and always assisted by
Something Radically Wise. Forgive and
cherish who you are. See yourself as
powerfully blessed, and you will see the
beauty in others.

*Today, I practice not judging others
or myself.*

23 *january*

. . . .

It's hard to let insights in, if you've locked the doors. Sometimes you are begging for clarity, just as long as it's a nice, tidy, respectable answer—preferably one that doesn't wear a boa, drag mud in through the door, or really require much. Are you looking for guidance that tells you how nothing has to change and you can get everything you want? Ask unconditionally. Let it rip. The heart speaks with closure to the open mind. When you're ready for *any* answer, you'll receive a jewel you know is yours.

Today, I am willing to open my mind to any insight.

24 *january*

. . . .

Sometimes I don't know an answer because
I can't feel. I'm numb, tired, hyper, and
haven't exactly been in my body in at least a
decade. Really, nobody's home. A hundred
genies could pop out of a hundred bottles
and, honestly, I wouldn't know it. It's time
to feel again. Cry. Take a hot bath. I remind
myself that the price of escapism is no escape.
So I'm willing to feel hollow. Because
everything I want is on the other side.

Today, I am willing to feel my feelings,
even the painful ones.

25 *january*

. . . .

Do the task at hand with the devotion of a
monk who beholds the *continuous holy*, and
vistas will emerge. Sometimes the Universe
has given you an answer. It's right in front of
you. Work with the client you have. Clean
out the garage and create a studio. Water the
marigold seeds in the blue pot. Love the
neighbors who come to the screen door.
Take care of what's in your midst with great
love. Don't wait for the next thing to come as
though it will hold more grace. Tend to the
work that you've already been given.

*Today, I tend with great love to the
tasks that I have already been given.*

26 *january*

· · · · · · · · · · · · · ·

If you want to experience magic, you have to
take a risk. You can read all the books on
parachutes. But you won't ever know the
feeling of true support, insane grace, and
wonder until you're falling through the air
and your parachute opens like butterfly
wings—just like all the books promised.

Today, I am willing to leap. I will know
support when I do.

27 *january*

. . . .

An optometrist surmises your prescription by
showing you the eye chart through different
lenses. Is this clear or is that clear? Is that a
letter *E* or just some splotch on the wall and
a trick question? You keep sampling until
you discover the formula. Same thing with
finding your right life. Keep sampling. Does
this activity light you up, or does that activity
light you up? Sometimes you have to look at
many things to see anything.

*Today, I am willing to keep comparing
and contrasting to get to clarity.*

28 *january*

· · · · · · · · · · · · · · · · ·

A Course in Miracles teaches, "Nothing real can be threatened." You will never lose a relationship, opportunity, or job that is truly yours. You will always experience health, unless it's no longer in your soul's health to do so. Nothing in this world will threaten your spirit. You are your spirit.

Today, I rest in knowing that nothing real can be threatened.

29 *january*

. . . .

Can you remember a time when you felt
brave? Or a moment when you felt alive—
and everything felt like it was in alignment?
Relish this memory. Gild it. Tell it to
someone or journal it in dripping detail.
This is a touchstone. It's an amulet. It's
ammunition. This time has lessons to teach
you about your real self. That moment is
more real than anything else going on in
your life.

*Today, I remember, recount, and relive
a time when everything worked out
for me.*

30 *january*

. . . .

What do you want to say to the world? What
do you want to bring to the table? This is
your invitation. There are so many who need
what you have. There are no powers holding
you back. It's clear sailing when you're clear.
And taking action, even in tiny ways, will
make you clear.

*Today, I ask myself, what do I want to
say to the world?*

31 *january*

· · · · · · · · · · · · · · · · · ·

You always have a safety net. It's not your
retirement account, connections on
LinkedIn, the oil well you tucked up your
sleeve for a rainy day, your gold mine, or
golden handcuffs. It's not the vitamins you
take or the Valium. Not even the love of your
spouse or parents, who, well, sort of have to
love you. It's the golden love you swim in
always—the ardent, irrepressible fixed love
of the Creator for the created.

*Today, I rest in the safety of being
infinitely loved by my Creator.*

01 *february*

. . . .

Finding your calling or right life isn't an
eight-step, easy process. It's not about taking
the right assessment test or checking enough
boxes to step into the wild terrain of a heart
on fire. There's no recipe. It's a bit more like
meeting a shaman in the desert and allowing
the power of love to blow your mind. It's
changing everything you think you know
about reality, one belief at a time.

Today, I am willing to change
everything I think I know about
reality, one belief at a time.

. . . .

For years, I trusted other people's opinions
more than my own. I felt like everyone knew
how to do life except for me. Apparently,
they'd all gotten the manual. Then I began to
listen to myself. I began to listen to the still,
small voice and gargantuan spirit within me.
This opened up an adventure without limits
or regrets that has even touched thousands
of others. Now, as an author, I guess you
could say I've even written some manuals.
We are all oracles of our own journey.

Today, I trust my own opinions.

03 *february*

. . . .

Real results take real transformation. The
courageous take their time. The committed
know quick fixes quickly disappoint. They're
not shifting their lives for the appearance of
success. They don't want a sugar high with a
backlash and a crash. This time they're going
all the way.

*Today, I take my time. I am going all
the way.*

04 *february*

. . . .

It's exhausting to "make your life happen."
Sometimes it's more "responsible" to let go
of your own supervision. Can you imagine
allowing the waves to hold you up and carry
you to shore without you kicking and
critiquing your progress? An inspired
wisdom can guide your every move. Where
are you trying to force something? Where are
you insisting "It has to be done this way"?
Be willing to be wrong. Become available to
surprise solutions. Lean back and float. You
can rest in the love and intelligence of a
brilliant life force.

Today, I stop trying to make something
happen.

05 *february*

. . . .

It's easy to love ideas. Sparkles, flashes, and
fireflies. But when you start taking actions,
you will stir up resistance, self-judgment, and
doubt. The resistance team muscles in to
break up the celebration. This is when the
real work begins. Bring your love into the
hard places. Steadfast commitment and
compassion are the big guns you need to
succeed.

*Today, I will bring my love into the
hard places.*

06 *february*

. . . .

I choose to believe in my desires and the life
I imagine. I will respect my instincts. I will
not call my greatest strength naïve or
impractical just because I've been taught to
value facts more than feelings. Feelings create
facts. Passion changes the course of history.
I handle this flame with care.

*Today, I respect my intuitions, feelings,
and passion as much as I respect facts.*

07 *february*

. . . .

I am realizing I am never going to "catch up."
I keep trying to nail things down. And life
keeps spilling out. Today, I give up trying to
get a handle on life. Instead, I am learning
how to breathe in the bird-song in expanse of
a meadow in the midst of a thousand teeming
tasks. I'm not waiting to rest.

*Today, I do not need to catch up. I am
not waiting to rest.*

08 *february*

. . . .

Trust each moment to take you where you need to go. You won't always have the same feelings or thoughts or perspectives. One day you wake up and new opportunities become available. Opportunities are like a carousel ride with colorful horses that sail around and around. When it's your time, you'll see your horse. You'll jump and fly through the air like a natural. You're always a natural in the right time. (From *Inspired & Unstoppable: Wildly Succeeding in Your Life's Work!*)

Today, I remember that in the right time, I'll see my opportunity.

09 *february*

. . . .

It's okay to feel restless. If you are bold, you
often know there is more for you than where
you are now. You were born to stretch
your wings. Don't douse this hunger with
rationalization or distraction. Yet don't make
your current life wrong. The life before you
is instructing your promise and flight.

*Today, I know I am restless because
I am called.*

. . . .

There is no safe life. Where did we get the idea that life was supposed to be safe? What kind of joy or significance has ever been airtight? Giving birth to a child? Taking a road trip? Kissing that handsome stranger? Give yourself over to risk. Risk is the only friend you have. Risk makes your blood flow red. You don't want a safe life. You want a life that is so full of meaning that even pain, if it comes, could never cancel out the love.

Today, I take risks that give my life meaning.

11 *february*

· · · · · · · · · · · · · · ·

You may think this is an ordinary day.
But today, someone will receive a diagnosis.
Today, someone will get a new job, meet the
love of their life, or write the song that wins
them a Grammy. So much will happen today.
Somebody is giving birth while you are
reading this. Someone is about to take their
last holy breath upon our spinning blue earth.
Don't think you know what's in store. Don't
miss a minute.

*Today, I know that nothing is ordinary
and anything can happen in a minute.*

12 *february*

. . . .

As an attorney, I was terrified to take the risk of becoming a writer. I kept thinking, "What if I fail? What if I wreck my résumé? What if everyone laughs at the idiot who flew too close to the sun?" Still, I realized that as much as I feared failure, I feared regret more. At the end of my life, I didn't want to look back with ache and wonder about the life that might have been.

Today, I am willing to take chances rather than live with regret.

13 *february*

· · · · · · · · · · · · · · · ·

What if you let your spirit run your life
instead of your fear-soaked brain? What if
you stopped being so suspicious of yourself
and just assumed that maybe you weren't
surely going to end up on meth, or miss your
train or one big chance, just because you
dared to be kind to yourself, for, like, maybe
an hour? A small voice inside is trying to get
your attention. Trying to eclipse your sad
conditioning. You are royalty and prophecy.
You have talents like no other. You cannot
know yourself and refuse yourself at the
same time.

*Today, I listen to the small voice that
tells me I have talents like no other.*

14 *february*

. . . .

There is invincible love in your bones. If you knew who you were, you would rush across a thousand fields to hold yourself precious. Today, let lovers unite. But most of all, let us all love ourselves more deeply. You are worth all the roses in all the markets and it doesn't matter who buys you flowers. It matters that you bloom within.

Today, I am willing to know that I am precious and loved. My love for myself is invincible.

15 *february*

. . . .

There is no outcome that will not bless you.
You bring the light with you. You're the
homecoming queen thinking she needs to
win the election. You've already won. You're
already chosen. It's already done. The whole
world is simply waiting for you to choose
yourself. It will wait forever with bated
breath. You are that valuable and necessary.
We all are.

Today, I know I've already won.

16 *february*

. . . .

It's not about staying in control. It's about
staying in love. I know this isn't easy to do.
But you can take the fun bus or the misery
bus, it's up to you. It all comes down to
letting go of how you think things should go,
and embracing the possibility that something
wise and beautiful is actually taking place.
It is.

*Today, I trust that something wise and
beautiful is taking place.*

17 *february*

. . . .

Your inspired inner voice is as real as bunions
or a bouillon soup. It's not putting your head
in the sand to believe in a higher intelligence
instead of mass consciousness. It's putting
your head in the game. Love is the strongest
power on the planet. You want results? Trust
your Inspired Self. It's a power and a presence
that dwarfs everything else. (From *Inspired
& Unstoppable: Wildly Succeeding in Your
Life's Work!*)

*Today, I am willing to trust in a higher
intelligence instead of mass consciousness.*

18 *february*

. . . .

Dare to want an "impossible life." Don't
get yourself under control and accept the
sedation of the status quo. Your pain is not
a lack in you but a flare of unexpressed
potential, ticking like a time bomb. The
golden-eyed jaguar that resides within is not
calmed by your retirement plan, your talk
of "someday," or the pretext that things are
"good enough." Your pain is the reminder
of your truth. It won't let you coast when you
are meant to crest.

Today, I allow myself to want an
"impossible life."

19 *february*

. . . .

You don't regret the past. You regret the present. You regret the past only when you're not wildly in love with all you are right now and all you are experiencing in this time. Change the moment before you, and you change how you feel about everything. You can't be in the wrong life . . . if you're in the right moment.

Today, I am willing to do anything I need to do to fully cherish this moment.

20 *february*

. . . .

You may think you have to have all the answers for you to be at peace. But this is backward. Accept discomfort. Make peace with unanswerable questions. Make peace with uncertainty, loose ends, and dead ends. Peace brings answers. Peace brings answers you cannot imagine while you lack peace.

Today, I seek peace instead of answers.

21 *february*

. . . .

I invite you to be inconsistent and unreliable.
I dare you to break promises to yourself,
and I dare you to make new ones. To me,
there's grace in showing up lopsided, showing
up fitfully, showing up sporadically. *Showing
up is showing up.* The dream-basher in you
pushes you into airtight commitments, but
I invite you to stumble. Start and stop a
million times. Whatever it takes. Ten minutes
at the gym. One breath of meditation. *Every
act of love for yourself makes a difference.*

*Today, I allow myself to show up
sporadically rather than not at all.*

. . . .

Trade in that label for a ticket. One explains
you properly and makes you a perfectly
conventional guest at a cocktail party. The
other is the price of admission to a dance
of no regret and no turning back. Sure, the
place between places is awkward and
different and people may look at you funny.
But freedom always enters ordinary rooms
flaunting exotic robes. (From *This Time
I Dance! Creating the Work You Love*)

*Today, I am willing to trade in my
label for a ticket to freedom.*

23 *february*

. . . .

A Cuban friend of mine taught me a quote
that translates: "You can't take from me the
dances that I've danced." It's my favorite
definition of security. Let the stock market
do what it will. Let our blood pressure rise
and fall. Our only security comes in how we
spend our moments. It comes down to the
love and joy we give, receive, take in—and
take with us always.

Today, I remember that real security
comes from the dances that I've danced.

. . . .

The "real world" is a collection of
regurgitated facts, rumors, and points
of view. Your spirit asks you to discover
what is true for you. There is no one static
experience. Do not navigate your original life
by someone else's findings. Why live your life
in only one "official" room of the mansion?
The mind repeats only what it has heard
of the "real world." Your heart has a ring
of master keys and will lead you through
the doorways of what's real for you.

*Today, I remember that the "real
world" is not a fixed or objective
experience.*

25 *february*

. . . .

I'm not interested in what you think you
can do. I'm interested in what you are willing
to allow the Divine to do through you. You
will be assisted in every way. Your gifts have
healing powers for you and the world. We do
not need your excuses. We need your voice.

*Today, I am willing to be used by the
Divine.*

26 *february*

· · · · · · · · · · · · · ·

It is not eggheaded to trust a Higher Creative Power. It takes courage and dignity. In a world of spiritual dismissiveness, it takes power to stay true to an Intelligence beyond your intellect. No one sees the invisible. Yet everyone will see what the Invisible can do.

Today, I know it is uncompromising wisdom that trusts in a Higher Creative Power.

27 *february*

· · · · · · · · · · · · · · · · ·

My coaching clients sometimes feel as though they "flip-flop" interests. They don't stick to one thing. But I know experimentation is part of the process of finding yourself. You don't want to stick to something as much as you want to uncover a wild joy or significance that sticks to you. Forcing a direction isn't commitment. Staying honest with yourself isn't "quitting."

Today, I allow myself to experiment and change my mind.

. . . .

Do you sometimes feel like [fill in the blank]
should have happened by now? Don't let
urgency drive the bus. Fear can't take you
to the miracle of blooming in your own time.
There is a spiritual synchronization that will
make you weep with gratitude. If something
isn't here yet, it's in your best interest that it
isn't. Meanwhile, something else is here for
you right now. What might that be for you?
Take it in. Surrender your impatience to
the perfection and payoff.

Today, I am grateful that [fill in the
blank] hasn't happened by now.

29 *february (leap year!)*

. . . .

Today, I give praise for the changes. The
economy is shifting and soon will serve more
of humanity. The environment is changing—
compelling respect and cherishing. Jobs that
crushed our souls are drying up. We are
entering revolutionary times where creativity,
spiritual depth, and service will now take
center stage. These are the times we've
waited for.

*Today, I know the changes in the world
are leading us toward healing.*

01 *march*

. . . .

Be willing to let go of being acceptable.
Instead, be impeccable. Stop dimming your
light so that others "get you." Shine your
light brighter so that some may suddenly
remember who they really are. It doesn't help
those who feel limited for you to stay limited.
We are all connected. And you have the
power to free us by freeing yourself.

Today, I free others by freeing myself.

. . . .

The inspired life ends drama. If you're
listening to yourself daily, you just don't
step on land mines, especially those that
are marked LAND MINES. You don't ignore
sadness or irritation. Or whispering
invitations. You're paying attention to
yourself with love and respect. You don't
need a big wake-up call. You're already
awake.

*Today, I know the more I pay attention
to cues, the less drama I'll experience.*

03 *march*

. . . .

Some of us have the guts to keep our minds
and hearts open in a world of pain and
publicized negativity. We have the guts
to reach higher when we're told it's more
reasonable to settle and resign ourselves
to compromised possibilities. We may be
demeaned because we respond with peace
instead of rage or hope instead of blame.
Rock on. We are the Presence of the
Alternative. I bless you all today.

*Today, I meet life as the Presence of
the Alternative.*

. . . .

Sometimes you have to do things when you
have no idea how. Something in your heart
says: *That's it. This has to be done.* Or maybe:
Thy will be done. Or maybe: *I'm done fighting.
I've come undone.* Either way, you're going
forward and you don't even know how.
Vagueness becomes aliveness. And that's
an exceptional path.

*Today, I am willing to say "it's done,"
and let the way reveal itself to me.*

05 *march*

. . . .

When I worked in a job I did not love, I'd collect this check that assured me that though I reeled through my life in an efficient stupor, I need never wonder about my significance to society. But those days lacked value to me. They lacked a connection to my essence, the part of me that walked in purple robes out in the sage grasses of poetry and possibility. In contrast, journaling, asking myself the most important questions of my lifetime, felt *honorable.* I was taking this time out to find out who I was and where my real life called me to go. (From *This Time I Dance! Creating the Work You Love*)

Today, I honor what I value, not what society tells me is valuable.

. . . .

You will never know abundance by holding
back your fierce heart. You will never realize
your wingspan by decorating your cage. You
did not come here to make due. You came
here to undo anything that mires your
full expression. Where are you choosing
temporary comfort over the ultimate comfort
of becoming who you are meant to be? It's
time to fly. It's time to cry. It's time to try.

*Today, I will not choose comfort over
flight.*

07 *march*

Your past is not here. It's a memory. It's a
fiction. It's a ragtag collection of ideas you
have savored. You are not the circumstances
you remember. Your spirit has never been
limited by history. The wholeness within
you cannot be changed. When you're ready
to have a new future, you will.

*Today, I step into a future that
is different from my past.*

. . . .

You are being hypnotized to define yourself
by the standards of imprisonment: standards
that make you feel "less than" while
promising you that you can and should
"have it all." I want you to use the standards
of liberation: Does this thought, desire, or
choice make me feel alive in this moment?
If not, it's a lie. It's a veil over the truth. Take
back your freedom. Take back your focus.

*Today, I focus only on what makes me
feel alive.*

09 *march*

. . . .

You may not have an easy life at this time.
But it's not because you're failing, falling, or
inadequate. It's because your soul demands
healing more than coping, soaring more than
just reaching cruising altitude. You may not
feel "fit" for this world. But that's because
you are called to discover your own
astonishing capacities and move beyond
constraints you once thought were real.

*Today, I know I am not failing. I am
going deeper, because I choose to soar
higher.*

10 *march*

. . . .

I am choosing to be devout instead of polite.
I am honoring my instincts instead of
conditioning. I am choosing to say no to
certain things, because a "yes, yes, yes" beats
in my blood for other activities. I am already
spoken for by my gifts. I honor my desires
because I know that my truth is a blessing.

*Today, I will say no to certain things,
knowing my soul has already said yes to
other things.*

11 *march*

. . . .

It's not about taking all the "right" actions. It's not about crossing *t*'s and dotting *i*'s. It's not about chemistry, genes, algorithms, and who you know or who knows you. All of this is superstition, even when it's called empirical evidence. The force of your Spirit is what prevails. Align yourself with your alignment. Love with boldness. Take flight.

Today, I love with boldness. I'm not worried about taking the "right" actions.

12 *march*

. . . .

If you want to get ahead, don't get ahead of yourself. Do you turn your fun ideas into something "productive" or force them into a money-making possibility? Do you start thinking you might have to do something you don't want to do? Get out of the planning mind and into receiving the colors of the garden in the moment. Take the future out of the equation. Follow the rushes of joy and light that can create a life you couldn't have planned.

Today, I keep my fun ideas fun.

13 *march*

. . . .

The magic is not gone just because you hit
a bump in the road. Infinite love is with you.
There is no world apart from love. Love is
all around you, and always has been. The
bumps are challenges to your ego, but not
to your destiny. There is only one power.

Today, I remember that the bumps
in the road are part of the magic.

14 *march*

. . . .

It's not an opportunity if it doesn't feel like an opportunity. If it feels like a "should," it's not your turn and it's not your taxi. Now just to be clear, I have accepted other opportunities that felt big, scary, and hairy to me. But they always felt like the time to take this step. I always had the sense that I was supposed to do this. I may still have felt a thousand butterflies inside, but I didn't feel a bowling ball at the pit of my stomach. (From *Inspired & Unstoppable: Wildly Succeeding in Your Life's Work!*)

Today, I do not act out of a sense of "should." If it doesn't feel like an opportunity for me, it isn't.

15 *march*

· · · · · · · · · · · · · ·

So many think their dreams won't offer as
much as their current jobs or life situations.
But dreams will pay you more. You have to
use a higher math. Tally the true value. How
much is it worth to you not to give your spirit
or the hours of your life away? How much is
it worth to you to be an example to your
daughter or son that love is more powerful
than fear? How much is it worth not to suffer
apathy, self-loathing, heart failure, ulcers,
or regret?

*Today, I tally the true value of my
choices.*

16 *march*

. . . .

When you do not have peace of mind, there's
never enough money, fame, love, or Armani
to satisfy you. But when you know peace of
mind, everything makes sense and falls into
place. Do not chase a "security" that always
agitates. Don't fall for the temptation to just
get that one other thing. Right now—realize
you have everything. Or you will never
have it.

*Today, I know I have everything
right now.*

17 *march*

. . . .

It's not easy to walk off the beaten path.
It takes guts to trust your way, when you're
not sure you have a way. The popular seems
"attractive," though you will find it ugly if it's
not your way. No one asks to be different. But
if you're asked, you must answer to this glory.

*Today, I am willing to choose in ways
that others wouldn't.*

. . . .

Here's how to take a risk. Decide it doesn't have to "work out" immediately. It doesn't have to lead to a preordained outcome. It doesn't have to end up making a million dollars. It doesn't even have to be "worth" a mention in the throwaway newsletter of your neighborhood. Follow the spur to do it. Enter the holy curriculum of listening to and learning about yourself. This commitment will lead, heal, and resurrect you. Allow yourself to be anointed. Remember, you risk more by denying yourself the chance to grow.

Today, I look at risks I desire to take as chances to listen to and learn about myself.

19 *march*

. . . .

It doesn't matter what you didn't accomplish yesterday. It doesn't matter that you haven't looked at your project for more than a week or a month or that you abandoned it like a piece of fruit in the back of the refrigerator and it has now grown spores and a small apartment complex of microorganisms. It doesn't matter that you think nothing will ever change or go right again. Just come back again. (From *This Time I Dance! Creating the Work You Love*)

Today, I choose again. I return to what is important to me.

20 *march*

. . . .

Spirit wants to flow through you. Where are
you blocking this connection? Do you need
to forgive yourself for something? There is
nothing you could do that would change
your worthiness of Infinite Love. I just
don't believe in a Spirit that is offended by
anything, while teaching me forgiveness.

*Today, I am willing to let go of any
belief I have that makes me feel
unworthy.*

21 *march*

· · · · · · · · · · · · · · · ·

So many people use "trusting the Universe,"
or believing in "God's plan," or "what's
meant to be" as a kind of pious reason to sit in
their rocking chair, nurse their wounds, and
wait for a rainbow, a paycheck, or a patron
to show up at their door. Yeah, well, my
spirituality is a call to vibrancy. It's got rocket
fuel. Because I do trust Spirit, because I do
believe that I am meant to be who I dream
of being, I take action. My faith gives me
legs—to go with my wings.

*Today, I take action because I believe
that things* are *working out for me.*

22 *march*

. . . .

It is on the invisible levels that we create ourselves and our lives. The sweetest declarations take place, mostly unwitnessed. This is where we decide who we will be. It's the moment we decide to go to the gym even when we're jiggling in Lycra. It's asking for a date, a raise, or a connection, while shaking and baking inside. It's showing up, knowing you're a great friend or rock star, even when no one shows up for you. Yet.

Today, I know that it's on the invisible levels that I decide who I am.

23 *march*

. . . .

You are always where you need to be. It's not
like there is a wicked brilliance only some of
the time. There are no lapses in the integrity
of a Higher Love. Today, pay attention to
experiences of support, movement, health,
or that which you would most like to receive.
Do not pay attention to what you are not yet
receiving. Your attention is your faith.

Today, I focus my attention on the
moments I am receiving what I want.

24 *march*

. . . .

If you feel there's something more for you,
you're right. It is not your wounds that hurt
you; it is your promise. It is the promise the
Universe made to you and you made to the
Universe. It is the thousand and one blossoms
that live within one seed. And you have a
thousand and three seeds in but one chamber
of your heart and it is too much to deny. It is
not your lack of life that torments you; it is
the presence of your True Life.

*Today, I bless the pressing on my heart
that calls me to my True Life.*

25 *march*

. . . .

It's all about the mojo. Wild success isn't about going through the motions. This isn't about your legs. It's about the light in your eyes, the fire on your tongue, and the sweep of your heart. When you're bouncing off the wall with voltage and star power, well, and as long as your hair looks good, nothing can withstand you for long. So study your mojo meter. Do your actions stem from desperation, or inspiration? Are you coming from fear, or love? Because where you come from is where you'll go. (From *Inspired & Unstoppable: Wildly Succeeding in Your Life's Work!*)

Today, I pay attention to my motivation. Am I coming from love, or fear?

26 *march*

. . . .

If you're wondering if you're "crazy" because
you can't just laugh at office or social gossip
like everyone else, without something inside
of you wanting to scream "this is not my life"—
you are not. If you're wondering if you're
"unrealistic" because you need expression
and passion even more than you desire
stability—you are not. You're the free kind.

*Today, I accept that I want expression
and passion, maybe even more than
stability.*

27 *march*

. . . .

Love is the only way I know to get over fear. I
have had to love myself when I'm in my most
unattractive stance—lonely or angry or bleating
like a lost lamb and stupidly sharing it with
untrained professionals, who look at me coldly or
apprehensively as though I *am* a lost lamb. I have
had to "love" my fear, as in not make it wrong or
try to shove its nine and a half spiky heads into
the garbage disposal while no one is looking.
It is a messenger and I want to receive its true
communication. I've had to learn to be kinder to
myself when I feel fear. Compassion engenders
self-communication, revelation, and courage.

*Today, I will be kinder to myself when
I feel fear.*

. . . .

Are you overwhelmed? Frustrated? These
feelings back you up against the wall and
bully you into eventual clarity. Clarity helps
you know which train to take, which man to
marry, which regimen to follow. A bigger life
almost always arises from the confusion,
eruption, and pain of a life that is evolving.
They are one and the same.

*Today, I know that my frustration is
leading me toward clarity.*

29 *march*

. . . .

There is a vibrancy within you that is changeless, no matter how much changes around you. The brilliance of your spirit can alter the energy, vibration, and even the physics of all your interactions. You have a Love within which no limit can withstand. These are the times we no longer look to find our stability and power in the world, as much as we look to bring our stability and power to the world.

Today, I seek to bring my stability to the world rather than seek stability from the world.

30 *march*

. . . .

You do not have to make a decision before you're ready. When you're ready, the decision will make itself. Ambiguity is not weakness. Forcing something is not clarity. The right decision is already within you. You are clearing away any resistance to this answer.

Today, I know the right decision is already within me.

31 *march*

. . . .

We have all bought into the superstition that goodness is a soap bubble about to burst. But I challenge you to think of anger, jealousy, and strain as a bubble—a bubble that will burst. It all depends on where you place your focus, which altar you light your candles on.

Today, I am willing to burst the bubble of being blocked. The goodness in my life is solid.

01 *april*

. . . .

I didn't want to be a "fool." I didn't want to
be a trailblazer, a creative stray, someone who
marched to her own bongos. But I was born
to stay true to myself. And all of us who stay
true to ourselves are too alive for conformity.
We are not radical. We are just honest and
uncompromising. And our love may impact
the trajectory of the status quo or those who
are not "foolish."

*Today, I will honor my need to stay true
to myself, even if I veer away from
conformity.*

02 *april*

. . . .

No one here has it better than you. No one else
can keep you back. You have a love that can
move mountains, investors, and teenagers.
You can unleash more of this flow by
consciously appreciating what is going right
in your present life. Stop looking over your
shoulder. Look into your own heart and find
something you dearly love about your life.

*Today, I want to see only the grace
of my own life.*

03 *april*

. . . .

Militant self-control made me act out. When I was anorexic, I'd diet and live on lettuce. But then I'd end up binging on, like, a thousand pumpkin muffins, but who's counting? My drill sergeant would kick in, saying, "See, this is why I have to monitor everything. I live with a maniac." It took me years to realize that it was my need to control myself that led me to excess. It was the barbed-wire rigidity of my willpower that caused me to go haywire. Finally, I learned how to navigate self-trust. This didn't lead to ruin and abandon. It led to self-love, dignity, and a coherent life.

Today, I trust myself enough to break my own rules.

. . . .

Today, stop straining, controlling, figuring things out, and pushing yourself to be the Greatest Version of yourself. Allow your True Life to find you. It always will. You don't need to work so hard to allow what has always been yours.

Today, I stop pushing and allow myself to be pulled toward my truth.

05 *april*

. . . .

Are you afraid of what you'd have to "give up" in order to live your dreams? Dear one, you are giving up so much—by *not* living your dreams. You won't be moving into the unknown. You will be moving into what you've *always* known—your element and that which you are born to be.

Today, I am willing to remember that going for my dreams is never a sacrifice.

06 *april*

Don't try to figure out your whole precious
life, especially, say, when you can't even
figure out what to have for lunch. It will drive
you mad—and it's useless. Listen within for
one next step or focus. It's always available.
There is always a next move. That's how you
lean into, create, and embody an inspired life
that inspires.

*Today, I am willing to open to one next
step, commitment, or perspective.*

07 *april*

· · · · · · · · · · · · · · · ·

You may not have as much money, fame, or ease as you thought you would have by now. That's not what's pressing to the soul. How much compassion do you have? How much joy or life experience have you socked away? Do you know how to choose peace instead of condemnation? Have you befriended yourself in this lifetime? These are victories that matter.

Today, I will focus on experiencing peace more than on seeking money, fame, or ease.

08 *april*

. . . .

In the times when you feel weakest, you are at the apex of your life. This is a turning point. Will you choose to stand for yourself or abandon yourself? Your future will reflect this moment. The future of your loved ones will reflect it, too.

Today, I will choose to stand for myself when I feel weak.

09 *april*

. . . .

Thresholds are places where the earth opens
up, the veils part, and angels and saints hover
near. You may be slim on worldly resources,
but you have unworldly helpers, secret
beekeepers and fire starters, who light the
world. Transition, if you choose, is a way
of being trained in the laws of magic. Will
you side with your higher intelligence, or
will you side with your darker fears? Which
part of you will create this next part of
your life?

*Today, I open to the presence of guides
and the light that hovers near.*

10 *april*

. . . .

Today, drop your need for outcomes. Drop
agendas. Drop your definitions. Drop self-
criticism. And you will drop to your knees
with gratitude for the possibilities before you,
already present and as sleek as panthers.
Enter this given, holy moment and emerge
into an inspired future.

*Today, I drop my agendas and enter the
given, holy moment before me.*

11 *april*

. . . .

Follow your calling. People will tell you it's
dangerous to walk out on the edge. But, baby,
it's dangerous to stay in the middle. Find
your true voice. You have a power in you
that is not of this world. (From *Inspired &
Unstoppable: Wildly Succeeding in Your Life's
Work!*)

*Today, I will stop watering down my
voice, truth, and talent.*

12 *april*

. . . .

Feel frustrated by negative people? We are
here to be the difference. It's not a problem
that "they" don't get it. That's why YOU are
here. You know something else. You've been
touched, called, marked. Others will heal
from your stardust.

*Today, I remember that I am here to
make a difference and there are those
who need me to make that difference.*

13 *april*

· · · · · · · · · · · · · · ·

I move forward without an exact plan, but not without a mission. I know that I am called to thrive. The Unimaginable Love that gives me my desires and dreams will also provide the means. That's as given as oxygen.

Today, I trust that the Source of my dreams will also provide the means.

14 *april*

. . . .

Maybe you've been disappointed because
something happened that didn't look like
"your bliss." You take your marbles and go
home. You rage against this circumstance,
this life, and everything coming down the
pike forevermore. Your tantrum gets in the
way of your birth. Closing your heart is your
only problem. Closing your heart stops the
deluge of everything you desire. (From
*Inspired & Unstoppable: Wildly Succeeding
in Your Life's Work!*)

*Today, I will look at: Where am I
raging against a circumstance? I am
willing to open my heart.*

15 *april*

. . . .

Don't be afraid to make a decision. Your
"good" is not in the "either/or" realm. Your
good abounds everywhere. An infinite love
goes with you wherever you go. You will
always know a next move. A decision isn't the
finality of it all. It's just one stepping-stone.

Today, I am willing to make decisions.
My good is everywhere.

16 *april*

. . . .

I want to help destroy your old stories. I don't
care what got you here. I care about where
you will go from here. I care about how much
you will reach for what you desire with faith,
intelligence, and fortitude. I want you to love
your dreams more than your reasons for not
having them.

*Today, I let go of one old story or several
that hold me back.*

17 *april*

. . . .

You are here to become less afraid: To grow
spiritual reflexes and muscles made of
diamonds. To flood and unlock the hearts of
others. To burn with thanksgiving and awe.
To slip past self-consciousness into true self-
expression. It all begins by paying attention,
without judgment, to what you really want in
any given moment.

*Today, I pay attention to what I really
want in each circumstance.*

18 *april*

. . . .

So many of us want quick answers to the big
questions of our lives. Premature structure
can give you the illusion of control and safety,
but in the end these limitations yield limited
results. You will be searching again soon.
Only your truth will satisfy you. Don't grasp
at polished solutions that leave you raw. Dare
to be raw until you're polished.

*Today, I am willing to be uncertain
and raw rather than manufacture an
answer.*

19 *april*

. . . .

There is something you can do today that will change someone's life immediately. You can listen to them. You can listen to how they see the world. You can listen without trying to change a thing. Listen to yourself, too. Offer reverence instead of suggestions. Listening is a deity that sits beside us with heat, belief, and grace. Listening changes everything.

Today, I listen to myself and others without trying to change a thing.

. . . .

You always have the chance to choose again.
At any minute you can get back on track. The
past doesn't matter, the moment you show up
again ready to make things right as of now.
Leave behind your ghosts. Bring your spirit.
It doesn't matter how many times you stray.
It matters how many times you return.

Today, I choose again. I'm back on
track as of now.

21 *april*

. . . .

When you serve your life's purpose, it doesn't matter what you think is possible. An infinite power knows an infinite number of ways to take you into the expression of your right life, even if you feel like an *extra*-slow deer in headlights when you try to come up with a strategy. You are not asked to decide whether or not you can have your desires. You are asked to decide whether or not you will allow yourself to want something more than what you currently know.

Today, I remember that an infinite power has an infinite number of ways to take me into my right life.

22 *april*

. . . .

In deference to the power we work with, we shed our saga, our discouragement, our battered attitudes, and our expectations. Today, right now, even with the project that has you feeling as though a fifty-pound sack of potatoes has crushed your butterfly heart, consider the possibility that *something uncanny can occur.* Do not underestimate the presence of love. (From *This Time I Dance! Creating the Work You Love*)

Today, I am willing to remember that as I face a place where I feel discouraged, something uncanny can occur.

23 *april*

. . . .

If you are planning your life from your mind,
you may be missing the plans of your heart.
Your heart is not impulsive or irresponsible.
It's not a pirate or a puppy. It's a complex,
multifaceted oracle, kind of like your therapist
or business coach on steroids. When you
listen to this guidance, the future falls into
place, as though a genius had mapped it out
all along and even set it to the notes of a song.

*Today, I listen to the instruction of my
heart more than the insistence of my
mind.*

24 *april*

. . . .

If you don't do what matters to you, you
suffer anxiety. If you do something you love,
you deal with anxiety. Either way—real life
will always require uncertainty. Go for
meaning and love. Make the uncertainty
count. Besides, love and meaning are their
own kind of certainty.

*Today, I choose the uncertainty of love
over the anxiety of ignoring what I'm
meant to do.*

25 *april*

. . . .

There is poetry in real life if you look for it.
A flash of a cardinal can disrupt your focus on
illness. The flavor of honey or the scent of
verbena can make cracks in the wall disappear
from your sight. In a business meeting,
someone's face will be soft, desperate, or
hopelessly open. Today, go on a beauty hunt.
Delve into the traces of wonder everywhere.
It's God's secret way of helping you awaken.

Today, I hunt for beauty wherever
I am.

26 *april*

. . . .

I have often doubted my inner voice as a precaution, wavered and hedged in the name of safety, second-guessed in honor of ordinary practicality. But it doesn't serve me. Yes, of course I'm perceived as rational. I'm even still welcome in some cynical, established, vociferous circles of people— people with dark circles under their eyes, who live their days and nights steeped in facts, fear, media, arguments, and data. Still I know this agreement undermines me. I'm not as powerful as I can be. (From *Inspired & Unstoppable: Wildly Succeeding in Your Life's Work!*)

Today, I step into my power. I do not water down my inner voice.

27 *april*

. . . .

What if the "other shoe" didn't have to drop?
Instead, what if the other one rose? What if
the first shoe sent down a rope for the other?
What if when things went well, you were
creating a baseline from which to soar higher?
What if things never went backward? What if
when you "lost" something, it was always an
invitation to expand your love, expression,
or sense of identity? Your life moves in one
direction always. It's always giving you the
chance to grow.

*Today, I know that things can get better
than my best experience ever.*

28 *april*

· · · · · · · · · · · · · · · ·

Happiness doesn't come from protecting ourselves. It comes from realizing the Essence within that needs no defense. You long to realize how supple you are. You long to move past false limits of every kind, pitch shackles and weights and canter free like a white stallion. You didn't come here to hide from the very situations that will catalyze your own expanding capacities.

Today, I am willing to face the situations that elicit a strength within me beyond what I have known.

29 *april*

. . . .

Are you tired of being around people who don't get the real you? Stop knocking on doors that don't open. There are others who are as hungry for you as you are for them. Right now, set an intention to be with those who affirm and expand you. Declare your desire for synergy. Declare, don't whine. Then stop going backward. Stop making dates with people who make you sad.

Today, I will stop spending time with people who make me sad.

. . . .

Are you trying to make yourself do something before you're ready to do it? Finally, I know my opportunities have my name on them and I don't have to shake the tree to get them, or hurl myself out of the nest before I've grown wings. Timing is natural and instantaneous. When it's time to expand, my instincts nudge me, and a next wind current comes. I am meant to fly in my own bright time. (From *Inspired & Unstoppable: Wildly Succeeding in Your Life's Work!*)

Today, I will not force myself to do something before I'm ready to do it.

01 *may*

. . . .

"Realism" is for those who may not have the courage to believe in other possibilities. "Realism" bludgeons many into a lesser life. Faith is hard-boiled sanity. Anything that expands your possibilities has more practical value. "Realism" is for those "who weren't born yesterday." Faith is for those who are born today. Be born today. Don't let the white-knuckled limit your potential. Chase the light.

Today, I choose to be practical by following whatever expands my possibilities.

02 *may*

. . . .

People who aren't in transition are numb.
If you're alive, you're in transition. If you're
growing, you're in transition. If you're
freaked out, you're in transition. If you're sick
of reading about this, you're in transition.
We are all shuttling from the known to the
unknown. We are expanding our
possibilities.

Today, I celebrate knowing I will never
stop growing.

03 *may*

. . . .

Every action you take toward your dream
is a brick in the temple. Every action is
a pilgrimage. Every action is the opposite
of dying. Every action summons the secret
helpers. Every action inspires new brain
chemistry and cell growth. Every action is
the deepest expression of love for yourself
and others.

*Today, I take action toward my dream
and activate more resources than
I know.*

04 *may*

. . . .

Take all the time you need. Your dreams are worth all of it. I don't care if it takes you ten years to finish that play. Or to work up the courage to speak, or to get on an airplane. Let go of your urgency. Urgency creates more fear and slows you down. Take all the time you need. It's always the right timing when you're doing the right thing.

Today, I allow myself to take all the time I need to achieve my dreams.

05 *may*

. . . .

When you obsess about needing to make money or have specific results happen, you drain your concentration, stamina, and creativity, and muck up your pipeline. Life will always reflect back to you your true motivation. When you're coming from fear, people start running from it. (From *Inspired & Unstoppable: Wildly Succeeding in Your Life's Work!*)

Today, I will let go of obsessing over my need to make money or any other specific result.

06 *may*

. . . .

Where have you become guarded? What broke your heart? I'll tell you what's breaking it now. When you stop trusting, you stop participating in life. There is no safety in "protection." Love is the only safety. Open your heart again, and you will see you were never damaged. My love to you.

Today, I am willing to open my heart again.

07 *may*

· · · · · · · · · · · · · ·

Do you fear that if you go after your dreams,
you'll be hurting others emotionally? Do they
depend on you to stay the same? Trust in the
harmony of the divine symphony, where
every instrument enhances every other
instrument. The truth of the flute reveals the
truth of the trumpet. Then repeat after me:
*I am never hurting anyone else by being who I
am meant to be.*

*Today, I remember that I am never
hurting anyone else by being who I am
meant to be.*

08 *may*

. . . .

We all go through periods of loss and
emotional adjustment, but we will never lose
the Source of all our Good. You can lose a
job, but not the intelligence, work ethic, or
other abilities that awarded you the job in the
first place. You can lose a loved one, but you
cannot lose the love they gave you or the love
inside you that attracted them into your life.
A lamp in your home may break. But you still
have electricity.

*Today, I remember that I can never lose
the Source of all my Good.*

09 *may*

. . . .

I'm one of those people who always got As
in school. I crossed my hands, did what I
was told. I would have taken the Olympic
gold medal for rote rule-following, should an
authority have required it of me. These days,
I no longer want an A for doing what other
people tell me to do. I want an A for
Adventure. I want an A for listening to my
heart in this life, for daring to trust the
marrow of my soul, for giving myself
permission to experience my true powers,
raw magic, and life on my own terms.

*Today, I practice listening to the
authority of my truth. I want an A
for adventure and magic.*

10 *may*

. . . .

Plunge into being the world-change agent
you are meant to be. Write your memoir.
Forgive your sister. Ignite your employees
or coworkers. Take your family on that road
trip in Ireland. Nothing will stop you, as long
as you trust the genius of your Inspired Self.
You are meant to flourish. It's your spiritual
inheritance. You have a guarantee. And still,
you don't get to choose the means or the
timing.

*Today, I know I am guaranteed to
flourish.*

11 *may*

. . . .

Part of me knows that "all is well." Another
part of me darts her eyes, afraid to trust what
she knows. Part of me knows I'm golden. The
other part nurses disappointment. It's okay
to feel this dichotomy. We won't shift into
an Inspired Life all at once. The apple tree
doesn't grow buds or blossoms instantaneously.
Several branches are dormant. In some
moments, the tree is part winter, part spring,
and part summer.

*Today, I accept that blossoming doesn't
take place all at once.*

12 *may*

. . . .

"Infinite patience brings immediate results,"
says *A Course in Miracles*. Today, I practice
patience. I practice knowing that when
something moves slowly, it is deep, lasting,
and developing generously. I practice
knowing that the Grand Artist takes her time
because she does not doubt the outcome and
has nothing to prove. I don't want a knockoff.
I want the Masterpiece.

*Today, I take my time. I have nothing
to prove.*

13 *may*

. . . .

There is no risk-free life. You only get to
choose which risk you'll take. I say bet on the
sure thing. Bet on love. Spend your life on the
road that makes you stronger. Going after
things you want, whether or not you get
them, makes you stronger. Yeah, baby, take
that in.

*Today, I am going to go after the things
I want, whether or not I get them.*

14 *may*

. . . .

Are you looking for a way out instead of a way through? Challenges stop us, enrage us, engage us, until we summon a wild power from the bowels of the will we did not know we had. Then we can never again mask our magnificence, even to ourselves. Others can hand you their power, but they can never hand you yours. (From *This Time I Dance! Creating the Work You Love*)

Today, I am willing to go through my challenge.

15 *may*

. . . .

You don't always have to feel up to the
assignment of "being great." You can feel as
murky as the bottom of a pond or as frayed as
the split ends on your worst hair day, which
does always seem to coincide with a job
interview. Yet you are still magnetic and
destined. Your feelings don't alter your true
nature. When you feel small, just be willing—
willing to be a stained-glass window, allowing
the stream of perennial light to flood through
you.

*Today, I am willing to allow greatness
to come through me, no matter how
I feel.*

16 *may*

. . . .

If you can't find your "purpose," find a way
to love yourself more. Find a way to forgive
yourself. Praise your very existence. Praise
your house filled with clutter, good intentions,
and papers you save, while, really, let's be
honest here, not having a clue as to what's on
them. Become the referee that rules in your
favor. Your right life will come from the right
relationship with yourself.

Today, I focus on loving myself more.

17 *may*

. . . .

Living your calling is the courageous path
of disregarding facts, statistics, and the past.
There are no "experts" when it comes to your
original destiny. If you are listening to the
Presence within you, there are no precedents.
And there are no accidents. You have never
been here before. Yet there is something
inside you that knows the true reality of
where you belong.

*Today, I listen to the Presence within
me more than to experts.*

18 *may*

. . . .

Today, I do not sing the dark cutting song of
lack. I do not hunt for desperation. I do not
curse my life. Today, I do not tell myself that
"I don't have enough time or money or health
or love." I banish these sickening promises
and spooks. I have time. I have resources.
I have will. I have spirit. I am love. What
I focus on, I hunt. This hunt is what I feel
and teach my bones. This chosen experience
is my life.

Today, I remind myself I have all the
time, love, and resources I could ever
need.

19 *may*

. . . .

Appreciate the moment and give it everything
you have. That's the secret. Our minds will
tell us, "Oh, but this circumstance isn't that
great." Our minds work in terms of big deals,
small deals, good, bad, right, and wrong. The
heart works with now, only now. The heart
does not evaluate. It connects and transforms
the space. (From *Inspired & Unstoppable:
Wildly Succeeding in Your Life's Work!*)

*Today, I will give every moment my full
attention and love.*

20 *may*

Today, lower your expectations of yourself. This won't lower your standards. It will help you thrive. When you feel safe, you'll grow. Take the pressure off. Otherwise, there's a guillotine hanging over your head, instead of a crown sitting upon it.

Today, I lower my expectations of myself.

21 *may*

. . . .

I am willing to walk forward with fear and faith. I'm not in control, but I am in the proximity of grace. I am not alone. I am not limited to the crude strengths I've experienced thus far. I am co-creating with a Universe that does not ever have self-esteem issues or a lack of horsepower or compassion. I am discovering unknown power within myself as I walk into the unknown.

Today, I am willing to walk into the unknown and discover unknown power within myself.

22 *may*

· · · · · · · · · · · · · · · ·

You're either listening to a power that has
no limits—or you're listening to a limited
mind that has no power. Yes, you can scare
yourself, but you cannot change your
fundamental birthright. Despite your doubts,
you are loved and infinitely creative.

*Today, I trust that I have a power that
has no limits. I am infinitely creative.*

23 *may*

. . . .

Success isn't the prize that someone else sees.
It's not the number in a bank account or the
number of awards your kids win. It's how you
feel about yourself behind your eyelids—how
you smile, rise, or bow when no one else is
looking. It's a sacred, private love affair.

*Today, I focus on what would make me
feel good about my life, just for me.*

24 *may*

. . . .

You think you should be further ahead. You
think you must be doing it wrong. But you
are standing on the corner of Inevitable and
Good. God knows where to find you. There
is nothing but AWESOME heading your
way. Ever.

Today, I know that AWESOME is
heading my way.

25 *may*

. . . .

Today, I will be merciful, hunting for
moments of kindness toward myself, like
spotting tiny blue robin eggs. Tenderness
breeds strength. I will become more of myself
by honoring myself for where I am today,
instead of where I think I should be. No one
else can do this for me. Nothing else will take
me as far.

Today, I honor myself for where I am,
instead of where I think I should be.

26 *may*

. . . .

Hummingbirds, often as small as a thumb,
fly five hundred miles to warm climates.
They follow instinct, not questioning whether
they can make it—or consulting pigeons,
parrots, or even ornithologists. Your instincts
will migrate you to your right climate and
environment, defying routine logic, and
using all of your complex, native abilities.

Today, I trust that I am migrating to
my ultimate destination.

27 *may*

. . . .

Loneliness is one of the "problems" with
growing. Sometimes, in order to connect
with yourself, you have to separate from what
you've known. The hollyhock pushes past the
earth and reaches toward the sun. Success
demands new alignment and, sometimes, a
seeming loss. Still, it's healthier to lose a
friend or condition than to lose yourself.

Today, I am willing to lose familiarity
rather than lose myself.

28 *may*

. . . .

If you're feeling unsettled by the unknown or
assaulted by change right now, remember, it's
a strength to be undoing that which no longer
works. This is progress, not mayhem.

*Today, I am proud to be changing what
no longer works.*

29 *may*

. . . .

When I was younger, "being different" cost too much. I did anything I could to fit in. I would have worn pants made of orange toilet paper if it would have helped my case, bowed to mediocrity, or definitely pretended to have flubbed an exam. These days, "being normal" costs too much. I'm not willing to fit in with the pack if it costs me my wingspan, my mojo, and my reason for being. I didn't come here to duck. I came here to fly.

Today, I am willing to be different from the pack.

30 *may*

. . . .

If you want a life of guarantees, you will miss
the point of life. We are here to explore.
We are here to love imperfectly and with
everything we have. We are here to rip off the
protective layers. We are here to melt, sing,
rage, and employ the wishes, seeds, and
hunches in our satchels. We are here to use
our lives, and leave with skinned knees, full
hearts, wrinkles chiseled and caressed from
exposure, and no regrets.

*Today, I am willing to love without
a guarantee.*

31 *may*

. . . .

I walked along a white beach in sun-kissed
Santa Barbara. I stepped into the water with
bare feet. The water shocked me with a bite
of coldness. Yet, soon, it felt joyous and as
comfortable as an old flannel robe. The
unfamiliar is often like this. Surprising at
first, then natural, easy, a second and third
skin, and as though you couldn't imagine
your experience being any other way. Seek
new comfort.

*Today, I dare the unfamiliar. I am
seeking new comfort.*

01 *june*

. . . .

Do you get distracted from what you really want to do? Perhaps you believe your dream is "just a dream." Please don't be casual with nitroglycerin. Your dreams have the power to repair you or tear at you. What do you really want to do?

Today, I will not get distracted from what I really want to do.

. . . .

The moment you are tempted to give up on
your desires—that's when the path truly
begins. What path will you take? One path
asks you to commit to your success, to give it
everything you have. The other asks you to
commit to the belief that you are powerless.
The commitment you make will determine
the lifetime you live.

Today, I commit to my success.

03 *june*

· · · · · · · · · · · · · · ·

You do not need to explain your journey or courageous faith to others. If you were giving birth, you wouldn't take time to make others feel comfortable and secure. You would be doing what your nature demands. You'd focus on the task at hand, the evolutionary impulse. You'd attend to your own needs. A new life will speak for itself.

Today, I do not need to explain myself to others.

04 *june*

· · · · · · · · · · · · · · · ·

Living your good life isn't about "getting things done." It's about being "undone"; letting go of unquestioned, limiting assumptions; forgiving past abandonments or judgments of yourself; and embracing your own peculiarities or distinctions, your exact situation and your gifts. It's a process, not a race.

Today, I accept that I'm in a process, not a race.

05 *june*

. . . .

Don't wait until you're fearless to do
something. Do it when you're trembling.
Experience gives you power. Experience
gives you freedom. Waiting shrinks your
life. You also don't have to do everything
at once. A tiny step ignites the alchemy
of transformation. One small moment of
willingness opens the door to everything
you want.

Today, I take a tiny step in a
significant direction instead of waiting.

06 *june*

Here's the big karmic joke of chasing success:
You can always arrive. After all, you didn't
come here to get gold from the world. You
came here to give it. (From *Inspired &
Unstoppable: Wildly Succeeding in Your Life's
Work!*)

*Today, I focus on giving my love to the
world instead of trying to get love from
the world.*

07 *june*

. . . .

Crazy good happens. It really does. It happens when you stop focusing on what isn't working. Take as many chances as a dandelion casting seeds. Stop putting pressure on every effort to succeed. Do something that feels good to you, whether or not it makes sense. You can't control just how crazy good this can get. Dreams do come true every day.

Today, I remember that crazy good happens every single day.

. . . .

One day you will look back and realize how
well you were doing in your life, how far you
had come, how much you had grown, and
how everything had always worked out
for you all along. You will see your own
grandeur—as easily as you see the beauty in
children, lakes, orchids, or puppies. One day
you will appreciate the soul's perspective and
discard the crude, habitual opinions of your
limited self. How about today?

*Today, I am willing to see my own
innocence and perfection.*

. . . .

One day I was feeling triggered. I swirled in old thoughts of self-doubt. I even started wondering if my positive attitude was a form of denial. Then someone walked by me. His T-shirt read, "Your ego is not your amigo." I remembered, then, that any part of me that attacks myself is not a part I want to take advice from. I was free.

Today, I will not take advice from any part of me that attacks myself.

10 *june*

· · · · · · · · · · · · · · · ·

Statistics tell you about the static. I want to
tell you about the ecstatic. Creativity turns
finite resources into infinite possibility.
Open-mindedness creates history. Advances
in science, business, and social justice arise
via passion, exploration, innovation, and
inspiration. Stay open today. Don't be a
statistic. Create one.

*Today, I open to the ecstasy of infinite
possibility.*

11 *june*

. . . .

Maybe you've felt like you're not cut from
the same cloth. You're probably right.
You're not "normal." You're not ordinary.
I'd say you're extraordinary. You're a voice.
You're a presence. And you are here to bring
something different to the conversation.
Don't let your difference isolate you. Let
your difference make a difference.

*Today, I use what makes me different
to make a difference.*

12 *june*

. . . .

A fearless life is one of learning how to walk
forward no matter what. We are choosing
from love, the power of being awake and on
fire. We are discovering what it means to stay
conscious. Going on autopilot is a suicide
bomber. It's trained to keep us the same. It's
wired to destroy or flee any circumstance that
rocks the boat. An inspired life requires the
radical will to go beyond conditioning. It
takes an act of mutiny to step into your
destiny.

*Today, I choose to be awake. I make
conscious choices.*

13 *june*

. . . .

When you are seeking to be inspired,
put aside your desires for money, fame,
convenience, and social proof. They come
later. First, seek undiluted magic. Do not
demand. Be humble, yet know you are loved
and worthy of riches. The Dispenser
of Inspiration pays unyielding attention to
nuances. The way you ask is the way you
receive.

*Today, I ask unconditionally to be
inspired.*

14 *june*

It takes so much energy to impersonate what you think others want you to be. It's so tiring to keep up an appearance or role. Why not drop the effort to impress or hide? Honesty is exciting. Want more stamina and kick in your life? Stop propping up something that doesn't stay up on its own.

Today, I drop the effort to impress or hide.

15 *june*

. . . .

As of this very second, I allow myself to
be blessed. I allow myself to be uncorked,
unabashed, and showered with delicious
good in every facet of my life. I don't need
to fit in anymore in the world of struggling,
suffering, complaining, belittling. I am going
nova and that's okay. (From *Inspired &*
Unstoppable: Wildly Succeeding in Your
Life's Work!)

Today, I allow myself to be blessed
beyond my imagination.

16 *june*

. . . .

Do you limit the success you think you can
have? When you limit what you believe you
can have, you'll limit what you'll do to have it.
I'd love you to dream crazy big. That's the
way to kick up the energy to create what
you really want.

*Today, I invite myself to dream
crazy big.*

17 *june*

. . . .

Maybe you're going through a time
of transition, and you wish it was over.
Everybody wants to rush through transition
like it's a bad root canal. But transition is a
threshold. It's a sacred life appointment—
the crossing from one identity or world to
another. Let go of your resistance and you
will meet uncanny power. Transition, if you
choose, is a way of priming for your next
level of potency.

*Today, I welcome the transition
I am in.*

18 *june*

· · · · · · · · · · · · · · · ·

Self-acceptance is the fast track to healing.
I thought self-acceptance was muffled, white
leather couch–therapist talk. Or New Age
vibrational rationalization. Turns out it's
penicillin for the soul, where infections die,
and healthy insights take over. What part of
your life do you need to accept right now?

*Today, I am willing to accept a part of
my life that I have resisted accepting.*

19 *june*

. . . .

Complacency kills you slowly. Beware your easy ruts. Your life can be more than idle conversation, or some additional zeroes on your paycheck, or (believe it or not) extra snacks from the pantry. It's never too late for a road trip, a degree in botany, an experiment in forgiveness, or the romance of a lifetime. Where do you need to stay honest, committed, uncommon, or true?

Today, I fight complacency and remain true to myself.

20 *june*

· · · · · · · · · · · · · · · · · ·

There is great fear in the world. But to me, tragedy is not "the news." It's a terrible exception. We have a choice as to how we respond to events. We are not helpless. We are the help. We are those who believe that love is stronger than fear, and that, despite irregularities and even some who have forgotten their light, our true magnificence will prevail.

Today, I remember that tragedies are the exception. And love helps in every situation.

21 *june*

. . . .

I am learning to honor my instincts
unapologetically. I am not a "control freak"
because I am intentional and discerning. I do
not have to give others "a chance" if it feels
like I'm compromising my intuition. I am
learning to trust myself.

Today, I honor my instincts without
compromise or doubt.

22 *june*

. . . .

Are you afraid of losing a certain relationship? *A Course in Miracles* teaches, "Nothing real can be threatened." You only want what's real. You want only authentic alignment. You do not want the shoddy manufacturing of the false. The "unreal" will break down. The natural needs no defense.

Today, I want only what's real.

23 *june*

. . . .

It demands a black-belt focus to fearlessly love
your life. It means being as conscious as a
rock climber scaling the side of a mountain.
It means choosing who you will be in this
lifetime rather than having circumstances
choose for you. This isn't about megalomania
or denial. This is about waking up to your
own fearless potential and that of every
human being. Because fearless love is the way
to rock everything in life: business, health,
relationships, and creativity. (From *A Course
in Miracles for Life Ninjas*)

*Today, I focus on who I want to be in
this lifetime.*

24 *june*

. . . .

Recently I drove past the skyscraper where
I worked as an attorney a million years ago.
I was transported back. My heart went out to
the young, terrified woman I was who was so
sad. I waved to her and bowed down to her
tremendous courage, leaving everything
so that I could have this life. "I'm free,"
I whispered to her. What do you want to
tell a previous self?

Today, what do you want to say to a
previous self? What do you want to
thank that self for?

25 *june*

. . . .

Here's the sexy, white-hot truth about your
creativity: It's a religious experience. It's a
transcendental adventure. It's losing the
stark lines of the daily self and entering the
transcendental kingdom. You come back
bigger. You come back full. You come
back with wings and fins and new toes
that seek higher ground. You never
come back the same.

Today, I am willing to explore my
creativity or any activity that opens
me to my Higher Self.

26 *june*

. . . .

Real life calls you to trust in life more than
beat its wildness down. You didn't come here
to control things. You didn't come here just
to manage. And you certainly didn't come
here just to count the calories in a dark
chocolate bar. You came here to discover the
astonishment of your desires and even your
"detours." You came here to trust in a
surrendered life, one that reflects your secret,
higher powers. This is your time to co-create.

Today, I let go of "managing" my life.

27 *june*

Sweetheart, you were born on a day, chosen
for you in all of time. You are the only one
who has your DNA and exact life
experiences, clustered like a honeycomb
within. Every leaf that has fluttered across
your path has prepared you for the life you
are here for. Every berry winked from every
vine at the exact right time of you walking by,
just to inform you of your promise. Do not
believe for an instant that you can compare
yourself to any other, for you are singular,
chosen, crafted, and divine.

Today, I know that I am incomparable,
crafted, and singular, as are we all.

28 *june*

. . . .

Self-criticism keeps you small and self-absorbed. You might whip yourself into remorse, but never genius. Creativity thrives on self-care and kindness. You can't do the work you love in the same way you do the work you hate. (From *This Time I Dance! Creating the Work You Love*)

Today, I feed my creativity with kindness and self-care.

29 *june*

. . . .

Being in transition doesn't mean you're
broken. It means you're breaking away from
the old—the world that no longer fits you.
It may seem as though there are big gaping
holes in your life. But it takes some room
to spread your wings.

Today, I know that being in transition
means I'm growing and spreading my
wings.

30 *june*

. . . .

My work here doesn't have to be oppressive.
I don't have to plod uphill anymore, dimming
my song or accepting crumbs and crusts and
bowing my head. I can keep my heart wide-
open and parade through wide-open doors in
a welcoming world. I believe you (Spirit) want
me to know your nature, and your nature is
not one of limitation or punishment or lack
of any kind. (From *Inspired & Unstoppable:
Wildly Succeeding in Your Life's Work!*)

*Today, I embrace that the nature of
Spirit is not one of limitation of any
kind.*

01 *july*

. . . .

Focus on your present chances, not your past disadvantages. Are you repeating history by repeating *the story of your history*? The past is over. It's a new dawn. It's a new you. There are infinite chances to reinvent yourself. The past is over.

Today, the past is over.

. . . .

Slow down. We live in a world of frantic
information and urgency. Nothing great
comes of fearful efforts. When you slow
down, you remember your core abundance
and resonance. You engage your grace.
When you are connected, you are magnetic.
The world accommodates the one who
is spellbinding.

*Today, I slow down and accomplish
more.*

03 *july*

. . . .

Holding yourself back from your heart's wild,
unfathomable desire is holding yourself back
from Spirit. Spirit is not excited by bland
compromise and insurance plans. Spirit
awaits you in the fire. Spirit meets you in
the impossible—not the predictable.

*Today, I am no longer willing to hold
myself back from my wild desires or the
love of Spirit.*

04 *july*

. . . .

A Declaration of Independence for the Free
Soul: I want to break away from the oppressive
nation of my old woundedness. I want to
break free from holding back my power. I no
longer want to live with only my low beams
on. I want to shine so unequivocally that
others decide to abandon their own shadow
choices. I want to break away from the
undermining thinking of the "realistic"
world—and choose some independent,
firecracker, celebrating-birth-giving thoughts.
As of this very second, I allow myself to be
blessed. (From *Inspired & Unstoppable:
Wildly Succeeding in Your Life's Work!*)

*Today, I celebrate my independence
from limited ways of being.*

05 *july*

. . . .

Every story you have about someone else
is really a story about yourself. You are the
storyteller. You are the hero. You are the
loser. You are the fortune-teller, the shaman,
and the oracle. You are at the center of every
story. You are establishing the meaning.

*Today, I tell stories only that empower
others and myself.*

06 *july*

· · · · · · · · · · · · · · · ·

Spend time with your Creative Self. Or for
you, perhaps it's another kind of Important
Soul Time. It doesn't have to be days on end.
But it does have to be *boundless*, a time away
from phones, e-mails, obligations, and
distractions. It may be awkward at first,
perhaps like a clumsy date. It may seem
forced, the commitment to making time, the
tidying up of other responsibilities. But it's
worth going through the gateways. Minutes
are worth more than diamonds.

Today, I commit to making boundless
time for myself.

07 *july*

. . . .

I want you to know that you are doing so
much better than you think you are. When
you're not inspired, you lack true perspective:
you think your fatigue is more real than your
fire. Or that you'll always feel as though
you're on thin ice. But you're just listening to
the hoodlums who spray graffiti on the
subway cars of your dreams. Those cars are
still intact. A mountain isn't broken by a fog.
When you're not inspired, you're not
connected to your strength. That's all. Still,
there are mighty forces with you.

Today, I know that I am doing so much
better than I think I am.

08 *july*

· · · · · · · · · · · · · · ·

Perfectionism is the spinster who tells you,
in mincing words, that she has "standards."
Well, I'll tell you, don't miss your chance at
love. Don't miss a chance to reinvent yourself,
step into the world or a conversation, or fling
your talent onto the main stage even before
you think you're ready. Everything gets better
with use. Nothing improves in a vacuum.

*Today, I am willing to take chances
my perfectionism wouldn't want me
to take.*

. . . .

The unknown can be safer than anything you've ever known. Sometimes what you've known is what other people have told you is possible. You've known the customs and conditions of the average. But what you don't know is the power of unlimited love, the range of unchecked inspiration, and the freedom of radical commitment.

Today, I trust the safety of the unknown. I trust something other than "common knowledge."

10 *july*

. . . .

Your gifts are not for you alone. Your love has
medicine in it. Any one of us who opens up
to the excellence of the divinity within us,
opens up for all of us. We are teaching by
what we choose to learn for ourselves. It's
where a new vibrancy enters this plane.

*Today, I remember that I have my gifts
in order to help others.*

11 *july*

. . . .

You can speak to the lower mind or the
higher consciousness in someone. You can
talk to the hobbled one within them, or the
king. You can speak to the gifted, or the
limited. Whoever you address will answer
you. And what you see in them, you will
strengthen within them and within yourself.

Today, I speak to the king or queen in
everyone.

12 *july*

· · · · · · · · · · · · · · · ·

I am priveleged to be a conscious human being with a mind of her own. I will not blindly adhere to "the rules" I didn't write. I pay attention to my energy. A medicine or program may work for some people, but it's not for everyone. My energy doesn't lie. I am lifted up. I am drained or unmoved. My responses are my truth. These are *my* rules.

Today, I pay attention to my energy instead of to "the rules."

13 *july*

. . . .

Circumstances fluctuate; your power does
not. Conditions don't matter. They have no
power. They can't vote. They don't sign your
paycheck. They are not essential to the plot.
Of course you can decide they are stop signs.
But they are really arrows, launch pads, and
sometimes simply the blank screen upon
which you project the movie of your choice.

*Today, I know that my circumstances
have nothing to do with my power to
thrive.*

14 *july*

. . . .

Investment brokers invest with detachment.
They do not bail when the market goes
down. They are responsive but not reactive,
or at least that's what we hope. As you follow
your dreams, you must master this discipline.
Let amateurs quake with fluctuations. Stay
the distance. Follow your deepest passion,
but not your emotions.

*Today, I follow my passion with
conviction and detachment.*

15 *july*

. . . .

When you don't yet have a definition or plan,
this isn't a lack. It's an opening. You don't
have a label, but you do have a ticket. You
have a ticket to anywhere you want to go.
You have a blank canvas. You can say yes to
any desire, sunbeam, divine invitation that
comes your way. *Something will come.* You
are in the exact right place where magic can
find you. (From *This Time I Dance! Creating
the Work You Love*)

*Today, I have a ticket to anywhere I
want to go. I stand in the exact right
place where magic can find me.*

16 *july*

. . . .

Why should you not embody bold grace and abundance? Who does it serve to have you be stunted? Your grace can raise consciousness and awareness and the level of love on this planet. We need you to rise to the light that you contain so that others can rise as well. It is not yours to worry about whether you have more good than others. It is your assignment to use the circumstances given you.

Today, I accept abundance, grace, and all my good so that I can help others rise.

17 *july*

. . . .

The real heroes are in the middle of things,
sweating in the middle of the night alone,
doubting the future, crying the tears of self-
doubt, burning holes in the ground with their
mad desire to flee. Celebrate the ones who
are making choices right now that others
will not see. Celebrate yourself, right now,
as though you are the biggest winner of all
time—because you are, dear one, you are.
You are sticking with the wonderful
and terrible confusion of creating an
authentic life.

Today, I celebrate myself for being in
the middle of things. I am heroically
sticking through this.

18 *july*

. . . .

Silence is not rejection. It's not
condemnation. It's not even about you.
But what do you do with the lack of praise,
money, or votes of confidence? Do you fill
in the blanks with ideas that damage your
stamina? Do you stomp on your own daisies
with heavy black boots? Keep sharing your
truth. Beam it from the rafters. Love always
attracts love in the end.

*Today, I will not take silence as
condemnation.*

. . . .

Want to meditate, write, lift weights, or tell
your wife the truth? Dive in. Go further.
When the "complainer" or "critic" or the
seduction of resistance kicks in, be honest.
Ask yourself, with playfulness, and no
judgment, "Can I stay with this activity a
little longer? Will this boredom/anxiety kill
me? Will hunger really waste my bones if
I don't get up to devour that brownie? Or is
this too much for me right now?" *Let your
truth decide instead of your resistance.*

*Today, I stay present with my higher
goal and present with my discomfort.*

20 *july*

. . . .

You deserve to feel secure inside, resolved,
and whole. Stop going it alone. Ask for help.
Ask within. Begin this vital communication.
Bring your hesitancy, your heckler, your
intellectual, your disappointed one, and
even the one who thinks you do not deserve
complete contact with complete love. But
don't deny yourself the privilege of using your
full strength. It's worth a thousand false starts
to start the most vivid relationship of your
lifetime.

Today, I ask for help from within.

21 *july*

. . . .

If you want to be happy, rip up your scripts
for other people. Burn the scorecard. Take
back the roles you assigned to those around
you. Leave if you must. But accept and bless
who they are right now—their flaws, pain,
and the journey before them. Let go of
demanding specific behaviors. Instead, relish
the spontaneous communications of love that
come to you unbidden.

*Today, I rip up my scripts for other
people.*

22 *july*

. . . .

Soul time is different from linear time.
It's a time of birthing, redefining, asking
fundamental questions, surrendering to a
mystical creative force, and healing any place
within us where we have failed to champion
and forgive ourselves. People who don't work
in creative time have a bit more of a simplistic
view and tell you that it's easy to get things
done. But look deeply into their eyes, and
glimpse the flatness, and you will remember
that some never question the value of what
they're getting done or at what cost. (From
*Inspired & Unstoppable: Wildly Succeeding
in Your Life's Work!*)

*Today, I know I will get the right things
"done" in soul timing.*

23 *july*

· · · · · · · · · · · · · · · ·

Just because you don't take action doesn't mean you're lazy or procrastinating. You may be listening to deeper forces. You may be saving time. You may be being honest about what you want to do.

Today, I know it is also action not *to take action.*

24 *july*

. . . .

"I need to be practical," my clients say, as
though growing into everything they were
meant to be would somehow be impractical,
like wearing nothing but a tiara in a
snowstorm. What they're really saying is,
"I want to stay within the parameters
I know." I recognize myself in every single
one of them. We are all longing for our own
magnitude, yet still clutching to decisions
that diminish us. Where can you trade in
your rationalization for creative investigation?

Today, I am willing to make unusual
choices that feel good.

25 *july*

. . . .

Take exquisite care of yourself and
spontaneous strategies, synchronicities,
and opportunities will match your inner
abundance. This is no piece of cake. It's
a piece of cake and a nap—without any
belittling self-judgment. It takes courage
and wisdom to be lavishly kind to yourself.
Believe me, this is not your father's
"productivity."

*Today, I practice taking exquisite care
of myself.*

. . . .

The hero's journey *creates* the hero. Heroes
don't skip steps, bribe the bouncer, or jet off
to lush destinations. That's tourism. Heroism
doesn't mark a change in position—rather a
change in self. Real achievement occurs in
our energy, in our chemistry, and in the way
we hold ourselves even when no one else is
looking. It's not the fluted bottle that makes
the wine. It's the fermentation. (From *This
Time I Dance! Creating the Work You Love*)

*Today, I honor that I am becoming the
"real thing." My changes are more than
superficial.*

27 *july*

. . . .

A feeling is a feeling. It is not reality. It
is not a decree. It is an energy seeking
acknowledgment. Bang the drums. Draw
loneliness or confusion. Grab your journal.
I know this to be true: Underneath every dark
feeling, a deep knowing abides. *This will be
all right*. It's inexplicable, yet undeniable.

*Today, with love, I invite myself to feel
my feelings.*

28 *july*

· · · · · · · · · · · · · ·

Don't seek to be inspired. Seek to be *present*
and kind. When you're not feeling purposeful
or excited, take the pressure off. It's okay if
you lay on this couch for a thousand years.
It's okay if you don't want to say anything
profound, hack away at creating a fortune, or
save the whales. It's okay to *feel* like a whale.
It's okay to breathe. It's okay to recollect
yourself, integrate where you've been. It's
necessary. Blank space is holy. Your excitement
finds you naturally. Your true nature is
purposeful. It is your birthright to shine.

Today, I release myself from the
pressure to shine.

29 *july*

. . . .

It's awkward to trust your love, yet devastating
not to. You know that if you turn away from
this sweetness in favor of reason, you will lose
your way to everything you believe in and
resign yourself to a shell of a life, haunted by
the truth you've denied. Let me cut to the
chase and save you sweat, wasted potential,
and years: It's worth a bit of discomfort to feel
more infinitely alive than you ever thought
possible. (From *Inspired & Unstoppable:
Wildly Succeeding in Your Life's Work!*)

*Today, I am willing to be uncomfortable.
I am on the path to becoming more
infinitely alive than I thought possible.*

30 *july*

. . . .

It is possible to know you belong in a life
of "something more" and to experience more
than enough right where you are. The apple
seed strives to become a tree that bears fruits.
But to do that, it receives the nutrients of
the soil it's in. Longing for more will keep
you stuck. Knowing you are growing will
free you.

*Today, I move toward my future
harvest by appreciating more of my
present circumstances.*

31 *july*

. . . .

I am coming to see that free time is not
indulgence, but a kind of vigilance. Knowing
myself and knowing my dreams comes from
having time. Without self-connection, I won't
have true direction. (From *This Time
I Dance! Creating the Work You Love*)

*Today, I take time out for myself. I will
never find my direction otherwise.*

01 *august*

· · · · · · · · · · · · · · · ·

What if you haven't gotten off track ever?
What if every situation has been your ally,
your guru, your training? Maybe you haven't
lived up to your plans. But maybe your plans
were too small, big, or cruel. What if just
thinking you're "off track" is the only thing
that is keeping you from feeling aligned?
Be generous with yourself if you want a
generous life.

*Today, I know my life is on track and
always has been.*

. . . .

Do not empathize with someone's weakness.
Empathize with their strength. The problem
is the least interesting part of the story. It's
just the device to dislodge trapped potential.
Always know that no matter what someone
faces, they have the opportunity to soar
because of it.

Today, I empathize with the strength in
others rather than their weakness.

03 *august*

True life is one dazzling mess. If you build a
house, there is sawdust, zoning complications,
budget issues. If you raise a child, there are
tattoos, illnesses, school expenses, and
household squabbles. Dreams are
adventures in the loss of control.

*Today, I am willing to lose control
for my dreams.*

04 *august*

. . . .

It's never a step down to step ahead.
Sometimes we give up "security" or
"appearances" so that we can know the
reality of excitement, freedom, and a security
that can't be shaken. It doesn't matter what
your life looks like. It matters what it feels
like. (From *This Time I Dance! Creating
the Work You Love*)

*Today, I remember it doesn't matter
what my life looks like. It matters
what it feels like.*

. . . .

Many of us have believed that if there's a loving Universe, then everything goes our way. But it's a rookie mistake, an unseasoned understanding of Transcendent Love. Transcendent Love is a presence that stretches us, grows us, dares us to be the most magnificent expression of ourselves that we can be—and deeply assists us all the while. Real love is bigger than our present understanding.

Today, I trust in the love of the Universe, even when I don't understand it.

. . . .

I see this all the time. Someone wants
answers, before they take a step. Yet it's
in taking some steps that the answers
come. Take one step toward your desire,
and you will have a new vantage point,
new information, new questions, new
muscles, and new energy. Even pain is a
communication. The mind is a vacuum.
But experience offers tangible clues, tutorials,
and eagle feathers and cherries that affirm
your path.

*Today, I take one step forward in an
area of my life where I want answers.*

07 *august*

. . . .

Your entire life is based on the thoughts you choose. The thoughts you choose are more important than the school you attend, the job you get, the wealth in your bank account, the talents you have, the love of your family, or the health of your body. (From *A Course in Miracles for Life Ninjas*)

Today, I pay attention to my thoughts.

08 *august*

. . . .

When I'm terrified, I work to accept the worst-case scenario. I call it Plan Z. I know if I can imagine surviving this anathema, which I can, I am free. The terror loses its sting. It's not that I'm "okay" with it happening. I'm not exactly welcoming homelessness or weight gain, mind you. It's just that I stop resisting and running. And running, hiding, and dreading are the fertilizers of fear.

Today, I am willing to accept the worst-case scenario.

09 *august*

· · · · · · · · · · · · · · ·

Worried about a loved one? They have their own destiny. They have a Holy, Radiant, and Loving Spirit that loves them even more than you do. There is never a time when someone you love doesn't have a bevy of angels by their side.

Today, I trust that the one I love is being loved and helped by Spirit.

. . . .

I don't need to be rational. I want to be alive.
I don't want to be measured. I want to be
immeasurable. I don't want to stuff myself
into a role at the cost of an idea. Sometimes
it costs too much to conform. Because it's
never really rational to choose a label over
a miracle.

*Today, I choose aliveness over
definition.*

11 *august*

. . . .

Do not look at yourself through the eyes
of those who diminish you. They are blind
with fear. There are those who believe in you.
Their eyes tell the truth. If you do not feel
loved by someone, they are not seeing who
you are.

*Today, I look at myself through the eyes
of those who love me.*

12 *august*

. . . .

When you are grueling through the middle
of things, can you write yourself a letter of
congratulations or buy yourself a small token
of appreciation? A totem of support? While
you're at it, celebrate someone else who is in
the middle of their evolving lives. Is someone
you know in the thick of a breakup, a layoff,
an illness, or daring to get sober? Honor
yourself and everyone else who is
courageously facing the molasses or razor's
edge of true change. We don't need applause
at the end. We need it in the middle.

*Today, I congratulate myself and others
who are in the middle of change.*

13 . *august*

. . . .

If you want to be creatively alive, emptiness is required. But most of what we call "empty" isn't empty. It's toxic with disappointment, weariness, and judgment. True emptiness is beckoning. It vibrates with invitation. Creative emptiness ignites a feeling of anticipation. *I can begin anywhere. I can do anything. What do I want to play with today?*

Today, I seek to empty myself of judgment. I can begin anywhere.

14 *august*

. . . .

In a Macy's department store, I saw a sign in front of a boarded-up construction area. It read: MAGIC IS ABOUT TO HAPPEN. It didn't read: DISASTER IN PROGRESS AND A LOSER CAUSED IT. So, let's place that MAGIC sign in front of the unpleasant aspects of our lives. Reconstruction guaranteed.

Today, I know that certain parts of my life are under construction. Magic is about to happen.

15 *august*

. . . .

It's wild arrogance to assume a static world.
And when you enter this moment with
excitement and love, you change the
possibility of every possibility. Learning
lessons from experience is wonderful.
Learning to be jaded is not. True "lessons"
empower you. They don't limit you.

*Today, what lesson from the past am
I willing to let go of?*

16 *august*

. . . .

Upset by something? You are still loved and every situation has purpose. Try not to shut down. Your response to the scene creates your movie. Your response will determine who you become in this life.

Today, I will respond with love instead of shutting down.

17 *august*

. . . .

Every curve of the road is guiding you.
Every tree knows your footfall. Every bit of
sky is whispering clues to you. A Mysterious,
Brilliant Love is drawing you forward,
rooting for you, investing in you, chanting
for your fruition. It is in the nature of your
destiny to lead you to your destiny. Every
circumstance you are in is a chosen
conversation designed for your good.

*Today, I know that every circumstance
is guiding me.*

18 *august*

. . . .

Limitation is Spirit calling my name.
Limitation puts pins in my sofa and lumps
in my pillow so that I do not fall asleep to
my own deepest longing. And, in the end,
limitation awards me a shiny, indispensable
credential in this world. Because, as I reclaim
my freedom in the midst of challenging
circumstances, I become a hope and light
to others.

*Today, I bless the "limitations" that
lead me to my longing and power.*

19 *august*

. . . .

Live a life of being called. Make the decision
to show up for every moment. Make the
decision to be alive for it all and let Spirit
decide the way it wants to move you forward.
Your job is to show up as a love warrior, arms
wide open and chest on fire, even when
circumstances look bleak, broken, or
"beneath" you. Do not be fooled by events.
A gift is always present. (From *Inspired &*
Unstoppable: Wildly Succeeding in Your Life's
Work!)

Today, I will show up for all circumstances
of my life with my chest on fire.

20 *august*

Forgive yourself or you block the flow of
instinct. You have always done the best you
can. Is there something you need to let go of?
An action you need to take? Something you
need to communicate to a part of yourself or
someone else? Please open yourself to the
reality of infinite opportunities. Nothing in
Spirit is permanently broken or barren. Let
go of the past and move into present time,
where you can choose again.

*Today, I move into present time, where
I can choose again.*

21 *august*

. . . .

You are worth the miracle. You are worth your dreams coming true. You are worth a new opportunity, an open door, another chance, a sudden windfall, or an unexpected manifestation. It happens every day. It's in the wings right now. Lift the veil. Bring it on.

Today, I remember that I am worthy of miracles. They are in the wings right now.

22 *august*

. . . .

When you're in transition, remember: It's
worth a bit of uncertainty to create a certainty
that does not change, even in changing times.
Fear might tell you to grab the lowest-hanging
fruit. I will tell you you're worth more than
what you can grab. Wait for your assignment.

*Today, I will not choose out of desperation.
I will await my knowing.*

23 *august*

. . . .

Now I don't know about you, but there are
times when I've thought that if the world
is depending on self-absorbed, neurotic,
poet-hearted me to be "a change agent,"
well, folks, we'll be going the way of the
brontosaurus, joining the bargain basement
of evolution's discards. There have been days
when I haven't been able to change out of my
sweatpants. I think God could do better. But
I'm wrong. I've been drafted and so have you.
We are here to share our light.

*Today, I know I've been drafted to share
my light, and it is powerful.*

24 *august*

. . . .

Change is love. It is the crossing guard who comes to take you to the other side of the street, though most of us go there dragging our feet and yelling for the police. Change gives you the opportunity to expand. When something falls apart in your life, energy is released. Allow that energy to now express itself in a more creative, accurate, and fulfilling way.

Today, I will stop fighting change and look to define and express myself in a more expansive way.

25 *august*

. . . .

Things don't take time as much as they take
willingness. You can begin now. That doesn't
mean you start at the bottom of the hill. The
minute you begin in earnest, you are there.
You are free. You are home. The right path
is the right result. The true walk creates the
remembrance of the true, and that's all you're
really wanting.

Today, I know that the moment I'm on
my right path, I've already arrived.

. . . .

Timing will turn on a dime. You are always
evolving. You are always growing, getting in
touch with new information and perspectives.
With the right opportunity, you feel the
energy to say yes. Readiness comes of itself.
You can't force it, fake it, or bribe the bouncer
at the door. One day, at the right time, and
not a second before, everything changes.
Every moment has its own original arc and
harvest. (From *Inspired & Unstoppable:
Wildly Succeeding in Your Life's Work!*)

*Today, I remember that timing can
turn on a dime.*

27 *august*

· · · · · · · · · · · · · · · · ·

One year I'd gotten a bazillion rejection slips.
No one would buy my writing. I grappled for
faith. "Bliss" seemed like a fantasy or, at best,
a restaurant or theater experience I couldn't
afford. At my bleakest moment, I decided
to give myself a gift, like some kite of mercy
to hang on to. I spent three days at a cabin.
I breathed in black night skies and stars that
could feed every hungry person on earth with
their beauty. Nothing changed in my life. But
everything changed. I felt loved. I could keep
up the good fight. Can you give yourself a gift
today?

Today, I give myself a gift.

28 *august*

. . . .

How much is being realistic costing you?
What if "realism" is just a broken scale, a
flawed measure of what you can be in this
lifetime? I've discovered the concrete power
of passion and creativity and it's paid my
bills, rocked my world, and opened me to
a sweeter reality than I dreamed possible.
"Realism" almost cost me the reality
I now live.

Today, I let go of being "realistic"
and negating my desires. I open
to discovering reality.

29 *august*

. . . .

So many times, I didn't speak my truth
for fear of being judged. But by holding
back, I lost the chance for understanding,
connection, and expansion. Always express
your truth and desire. Some may judge you.
But there are others who will receive you and
make you feel as though you are standing in
the sun. You will have your people.

*Today, I share my truth with others
because I want the chance to connect
and expand.*

30 *august*

. . . .

Your relationship with yourself is the most precious resource in your life. Are you walking around with a bitter troll? Or are you spending the day with an advocate who cherishes and champions you? Nothing in life will replace a lack of self-love. And nothing in life can take you down when you have it.

Today, I am willing to cherish and champion myself. Nothing in life replaces self-love.

31 *august*

. . . .

Remember that what you need needs you. The savvy publicist needs a rock-star book to represent. People with back pain need the massage therapist, who needs clients. The love of your life craves a love like yours to come into his or her life. This is one big collaboration. It's a flea market with a guarantee. Your need is part of the plan.

Today, I remember the person or organization I need needs me, too.

01 *september*

. . . .

Today, I practice receiving. I do not reject any conversation, cancellation, disturbance, or shift in my plans. I pay attention to a higher love seeded in every encounter. I behold metaphors, transmissions, and messengers of every kind. Everything comes alive in my presence as I am present to being alive.

Today, I practice receiving the flow and communication of this day.

. . . .

We're in times of the greatest changes, to help
us make our greatest changes. It's evolution's
love song to itself. The unpredictable forest
fire clears out deadwood to encourage wild
new growth. Become a change agent, one
who changes the planet, by changing the
definition of who you think you are and what
you think is possible. The times are ready for
you now.

*Today, I am willing to become a change
agent. The times are ready for me now.*

03 *september*

· · · · · · · · · · · · · · · ·

When you're tired, you don't feel creative,
hopeful, capable, or blessed. You can't touch
the light or depths. Rest is the first step to
flight. Our culture runs us ragged. Go
against the grain. Don't be so "productive."
Rest and let love's sunlight melt the clouds
in your soul.

*Today, I am willing to rest. I know that
rest leads to productivity and flight.*

04 *september*

· · · · · · · · · · · · · · ·

You do not need to know how to do
something in order to do it. There is an
Instinctive Intelligence within you that will
impel you to fruition. You will grow. You will
heal. You will alight on sudden outcroppings
of insight. You will meet all who advance
your direction. And you may not even believe
this. Still, following your heart's desire is
not a path of control. It is a journey of
co-creation.

*Today, I am willing to pursue my true
direction even when I don't know how
to make it happen. I will follow where
I'm led.*

05 *september*

· · · · · · · · · · · · · ·

It's great to have intentions. But it's
imperative to take steps toward what is
important to you. Steps will change your life.
A meager step unlatches creative propensities,
momentum, held-back emotions, and energy.
There are no small steps. Honoring your
essence is always huge.

*Today, I will take a small step toward
what is most important to me.*

· · · · · · · · · · · · · · · ·

Fear will not go away because you have
enough money in the bank or you're in the
right relationship. Fear leaves only when
love enters. It's not about changing our
circumstances. It's about changing our
commitment to love. It's about focusing
on giving more than getting. Focus on
appreciating more and insecurities and
doubts evaporate. What can you love today?

Today, I am willing to ease my
insecurities by focusing on loving
more. What can I love today?

. . . .

Achievement without self-love is empty.
Goals without flexibility and breathing room
are sterile punishments. I am learning that
how I hold my own hand on this journey
determines the quality and feeling of success
I experience. I don't want to "arrive" anywhere
without my own friendship and self-love.

*Today, I hold my own hand in every
pursuit.*

08 *september*

. . . .

Give yourself time to find your passion, your
groove, your strategy, your voice, or your
life's work. Take the pressure off it having to
happen two days ago—in a New York minute,
in a big, flaring, obvious King Kong way.
Give it your lifetime. Set out pails to catch
each raindrop. You will catch a river. Without
pressure, yet with focus, sanity and truth will
lead the way.

*Today, I give myself all the time I need
to find my groove.*

· · · · · · · · · · · · · · · · ·

Feeling anxiety? You are not in the present
moment. Fear comes when we imagine a
future that is not here or replay memories
or upsets from the past. Slow your breathing
down. Receive this moment as it is, not
asking it to change. Receive its sustenance,
surprises, companionship, and dimension.
Spirit is here.

*Today, I focus only on the present
moment. It is an oasis of safety.*

10 *september*

· · · · · · · · · · · · · · ·

When it comes to creating my right life,
I would have saved a lot more time if I'd
had less fear. I'd have paid attention to the
moment in front of me, as though it offered
me a once-in-a-lifetime opportunity or
training course. Because every moment does.
Yet part of me always wanted to rush the
process, hitch a ride that wasn't mine, and
speed into the center of Glitz Town like a
gambler desperate for a win. Now I only want
the gold that comes delivered to my door.
(From *Inspired & Unstoppable: Wildly
Succeeding in Your Life's Work!*)

*Today, I pay attention to the once-in-a-
lifetime opportunity in front of me.*

11 *september*

. . . .

There will always be storms in life.
The unpredictable will swoop into your
experience, knock out power lines, crush
the daisies, cheat on you, and threaten your
dreams. But there is a Power within you that
never wavers. Conditions do not create your
spirit. Your spirit creates your experience
of conditions.

*Today, I embrace storms. I know that
nothing can change my spirit.*

12 *september*

. . . .

Your small self lies. It tells you: You'll always
be wounded. You will always be stuck. But I
will tell you that if you keep taking tiny steps
forward, humming love songs to yourself all
the way, calling upon the guidance of a
Brilliant Love, you will experience a lifting
and a life you never thought possible. Honey,
you are going places, even as we speak.

Today, I let go of what my small self
believes about me.

13 *september*

· · · · · · · · · · · · · · ·

A big fat inspired life requires us to listen to
our bones more than to the Dow Jones. We
are grounded in the feelings of homecoming,
attraction, quickening, and alignment more
than momentary facts. We are emerging into
power rather than seeking immediate control.
It takes practice to become faithful and alive.

*Today, I am emerging into power
rather than seeking immediate control.*

14 *september*

· · · · · · · · · · · · · · · ·

Sometimes we don't act because our souls
know it's not the right time or right thing.
It's not that we're unambitious or missing
some essential wiring. It's that we're
intricately guided. Fear tries to push us.
Love will wait until we're ready—because
only our readiness *makes it* the right time.

Today, I know I will act in the
right time.

15 *september*

. . . .

Trust your brilliance more than you trust
your doubt. The only reason negativity
sounds "real" is because we've heard it more.
But then, there are more people who don't
dare to act on their dreams than those who
do. Dreamers speak a different language.

*Today, I practice trusting my brilliance
more than my doubt.*

16 *september*

· · · · · · · · · · · · · · · ·

Let go of your hunger for major outcomes. Welcome tiny shifts. All my major successes have come from consistent, flimsy, incremental steps. Big leaps are flashy. But real success, inspired success, isn't a package that falls from the sky. It's a way of being that's awakened in you over time. Are you discounting your own progress because it isn't visible or definable in a certain way?

Today, I celebrate my tiny shifts and incremental progress.

17 *september*

. . . .

You can't force yourself into enlightenment,
or pole-vaulting into change. You will take a
quantum leap in your own seasonable way.
You will spring to life when smallness hurts
too much. Grace is natural. It's involuntary.
It's not something you make happen.

Today, I trust that I will take a
quantum leap naturally.

18 *september*

. . . .

During a transition time, you can feel crazy, damaged, and isolated. But if you really want to feel crazy, damaged, and isolated, turn to family members or friends who may not understand your journey and ask them for support. It's natural to want certain people to be there for you. But not everyone knows the way of going nova. Seek those who do. (From *This Time I Dance! Creating the Work You Love*)

Today, I do not seek support from those who do not understand my journey.

19 *september*

. . . .

Want the answer to fretting, anxiety,
or feeling as though you're not getting
anywhere? Start loving fully. Create a gift
for someone lonely. Write a gratitude letter
to a colleague, cousin, or neighbor. Or delve
into a project with savage devotion, like a
firefighter attending flames. Leave no room
for questions. Get so busy loving fully, you
don't notice anything else.

*Today, I love so fully, I don't notice
anything else.*

20 *september*

. . . .

If you're in transition, honor this sacred
passage in your life. Sure, you feel nervous
or frightened. You are learning. You have left
behind easy competency. And now you brave
the unsettling immensity of expansion. You're
a small plant in a bigger pot. You feel small
because you're growing past your smallness.

*Today, I remind myself that I feel small
because I'm in a bigger pot.*

21 *september*

. . . .

Get off the beaten path if you want to
experience a life with a heartbeat. There's
an avalanche of advice on how to be average.
But it takes courage to detour into excellence
and awe.

Today, I am willing to explore the
fringes of an uncommon life.

22 *september*

. . . .

I have always wanted a savior, a patron, a champion, or a cheerleader for my talent. Instead, I have become for myself everything I was looking for. I realized I couldn't expect someone else to invest in me, if I hadn't invested in myself. So I went first. I cast the first coin. I'll cast the last one, too. I've got my buy-in.

Today, I am willing to be my own patron or champion. I will invest in myself and my dreams.

. . . .

We pray to stand on the pinnacle.
The Universe answers. It places us at the
trailhead. "I don't want this climb," we
whine. But the Universe knows the pinnacle
means nothing without the experience of the
hike. Our answers often look like setbacks or
miscalculations. But they are placements of
mercy, instruction, possibility, and progress.

*Today, I remember that every "setback"
is taking me to the pinnacle.*

24 *september*

. . . .

Do not believe your fear. You will not be
stuck forever. Things will shift. The way
will open. This is a Universe of Unceasing
Abundance. The only reason it's hard to trust
is because you keep focusing on what you
believe went wrong. There is another story.
There is another storyteller. Walk past any
voice that would deny you hope. It is only
your perspective that blocks your perfect
passage.

*Today, I will focus my attention on
what has gone right in my life.*

25 *september*

. . . .

You can always choose healthfully for yourself and, until you do, you will be tired. It's the lack of commitment to yourself that creates exhaustion. Stay powerful. Don't let exhaustion make more choices that create exhaustion. Stay trustworthy and impeccable in small choices.

Today, I will choose healthfully for myself. I will stay present and impeccable in my self-care.

26 *september*

· · · · · · · · · · · · · · ·

Pay attention to the nuances of what you feel.
It's so easy to skate over slight sparks, signals,
and for some of you (you know who you are)
bulldozers. Don't discount yourself. Your
truth is vital. Consequential. One of a kind.
You are receiving communication at all times.
The messages shift and deepen as you go on.
Listen ceaselessly.

*Today, I pay attention to the nuances
of what I feel.*

27 *september*

. . . .

Your Muse will not come into a room if
you've brought in expectations. She will
not enter a room secretly crowded with
surveyors, actuaries, accountants, and
salesmen. Believe me, she smells a calculator
in the room and will have nothing to do with
you. You have to come alone. You have to
come with curiosity and bare feet. You may
turn your inspiration into profit centers
later. But meanwhile, don't monetize the
butterflies. You must court inspiration on
inspiration's terms.

*Today, I open to inspired ideas without
rushing to evaluate them.*

28 *september*

. . . .

Life is relentless and challenging at times.
Maybe you've noticed. You are going to feel
like you got left behind while everyone else
went on a road trip or globe-trotting and
sent postcards. You are going to want to
judge yourself for not being further ahead,
especially when you've just binged on
brownies, and then read other people's savvy
tweets. I don't recommend a whip when
you're feeling hobbled. I suggest you explore
a hundred dimensions of compassion.

*Today, when I am tempted to feel as
though I'm not where I want to be in
life, I explore compassion.*

29 *september*

. . . .

Self-love is the quickest route to dynamic,
time-saving, original genius. You can't
criticize yourself and listen to fearless,
unexpected directions at the same time.
Start becoming conscious and treating
yourself with unconditional positive regard
as an active practice. Become a divining rod
for the divine.

*Today, I cultivate an active practice
of self-love.*

30 *september*

· · · · · · · · · · · · · · · ·

If you know you don't belong where you
are, you are right. Your skin doesn't itch
with the need to be muted, but with the need
to be obeyed. The world that baits you is real.
Your temptation is your ticket. It's not a tiny
spark meant to be stamped out before it
catches fire and burns down what you really
do not want. It's your rite of passage. It's your
birthright. It's your blood calling you with
ancestry and with future.

*Today, I remember that my temptation
is my ticket.*

01 *october*

. . . .

Some will say you are too big for your
britches and you will know you are, even
now, still growing. You cannot be content in
places that dwarf your spirit, that douse your
spark, that force you to bend down, speak
softly, and nod your head when you want to
shriek your fury and desire and hunger.

*Today, I realize I am not meant to be
content in places that dwarf my spirit.*

. . . .

When you do not speak, the thousand stars
that lay upon your tongue slide back down
your throat only to be swallowed one by one,
jagged, pointed, and weighing more than
planets. When we swallow the truth, we turn
our bodies into graveyards. What truth do
you want to share today?

Today, I speak my truth.

03 *october*

Are you compromising what you really want?
You cannot settle for a half-life because it will
hurt you more than no life. A half-life is no
life for you, even while others praise your
name. Approval won't keep you alive for long
when self-rejection lives in your bloodstream.

Today, I will not settle for approval at
the price of self-rejection.

04 *october*

· · · · · · · · · · · · · · · ·

If you are wondering why you can't just be
like everyone else, it's because you can't. You
were made with free blood and electrons that
whir inside you like lights, whispers, and
promises. You may know you were meant
to write screenplays, heal animals, traipse
across the world, or pattern the codes of
technology into magic wands. You may know
you came here to make a difference, and that,
dear one, always makes you different.

*Today, I am willing to accept what
makes me different.*

05 *october*

. . . .

I'm going to ask you to trust in your life—
more than in your script. You are always
where you need to be. It's not like the
Universe dropped your call. Your wise
eternal inner self didn't fall asleep at the
wheel or start playing for the other team.
You're still plugged in to power and flow.
(From *Inspired & Unstoppable: Wildly
Succeeding in Your Life's Work!*)

*Today, I will trust in my life more
than in my script. I am always
where I need to be.*

. . . .

Your work is not to make yourself be brilliant—but to allow the brilliance to flow through you. Your work is not to make circumstances happen, but to see what's already happening in your current circumstances. It's a co-creative way to live. It's the only way to *live*.

Today, I pay attention to what is happening for me already. I witness the brilliance flowing in my life.

07 *october*

. . . .

Stop this moment. Someone is unbearably
frightened. Someone is feeling as alone as the
moon. Someone is feeling like their dream
won't come true. Someone is packing it
up. As you read these words, feel your
compassion. Become a divining rod of grace.
Send your love out into the Universe. Now
allow yourself to receive what you have given.

*Today, I send love out into the Universe
wherever it is needed.*

08 *october*

. . . .

When you let go of a career or marriage, you
do not lose that identity. You expand your
identity. You take everything with you. You
may leave behind a role, but you do not leave
behind your strength. You are still everything
you've ever been—and now can explore and
express more of who you are called to become.

*Today, I am willing to leave behind
old identities and roles and take my
strength, love, and experience with me.*

09 *october*

. . . .

Sometimes you have to act when you're not inspired. You have to experiment. Visit an online dating site. Sign up for an acting class or a course in social media. Dare. Stir the pot. Do it begrudgingly, but do it. You may start off numb, but acting on behalf of your True Self will release your bottled energy. Application leads to inspiration.

Today, I take an action on behalf of my real life, whether or not I feel like it.

10 *october*

· · · · · · · · · · · · · · · ·

Do you feel like others don't "get" you or
your deepest desires? Do not take advice
from unhappy people. Why allow someone
who isn't living their dreams to tell you
how to live yours? Never limit your destiny
according to someone else's resignation.
Or their research. You were born with
radical powers.

*Today, I will not limit my destiny based
upon anyone else's resignation.*

11 *october*

. . . .

There is no comfort in clinging to what has been. Your "comfort zone" turns dull or even perilous. You are meant to spread your wings. You are more than you know. You discover new dexterity and the panorama of vision midflight. Life thrusts you out of the nest—because you're ready and your good will not be denied.

Today, I am willing to spread my wings and discover miracles midflight.

12 *october*

· · · · · · · · · · · · · · · ·

I used to feel sad when trees lost their leaves.
Now I see it as a time of abundance and
power. The trees drop their leaves because
they have reached the pinnacle of their
expression, and now they are willing to
reach further. Autumn is a festival of
casting off high notes and prior growth—and
an unmistakable invitation to a new life.

*Today, I let go of an old expression
of myself.*

13 *october*

. . . .

Sometimes we want so much for other people
that we limit them with our own expectations.
We think it's up to us to fix or help them. But
that can make them feel diminished. Set them
free. Trust their spirit. Witness their strength,
not their limitations. You do not know the
path they need to take. But you can be the
love that goes with them.

*Today, I set everyone free. I see only the
strength in them.*

. . . .

"How do I help my mother or husband or friend get this stuff?" students ask. I know they want magic words to pass on. "Become the light," I say. Let your own eyes shine with freedom. "Be with" your loved one in wholeness, acceptance, and wonder. In the presence of love, everyone gets what they need in their own language.

Today, I remember that in the presence of love, everyone gets what they need in their own language.

15 *october*

. . . .

When you don't know what you want, it's
because you're listening to a voice inside that
says: *"You can't have it. It's not practical. It's
stupid."* Yet the moment you suspend these
misguided ideas, you will know what you
want—and the certainty of your clarity
will be the fuel that gets you where you
want to go.

*Today, I am willing to suspend all
negating voices within me so that I
can name and honor what I want.*

16 *october*

. . . .

It's easy to lose faith. It's easy to feel small. It's easy to doubt your life. But these are all just careless, burdening thoughts. Rise up anyway. Learn to be independent of your own dismissive opinion. I haven't always had faith when I moved forward. I've gained faith by moving forward.

Today, I gain faith by moving forward.

17 *october*

. . . .

Your good is not as fragile as you think. It doesn't matter if you're tired. It doesn't matter if you don't think the "right thoughts" for ten minutes or ten days. It doesn't matter if you forget to say a prayer. Your spirit is stronger than fluctuations. Your True Nature always prevails.

Today, I trust that my spirit is stronger than my moods or habits.

18 *october*

· · · · · · · · · · · · · · · ·

When you ache for a life you do not have, you are not weak, but strong. You know who you really are. You burn for your truth, not a fantasy. It's not your circumstances that define you. It's the strength of your desire.

Today, I know I ache for my reality, not a passing fantasy.

19 *october*

. . . .

How did the best things in your life happen?
What were you doing/thinking/eating for
breakfast before they did? What weren't you
doing? Reflect on your personal breakthrough
times of ease, feeling at home in your own
skin, unexpected opportunities, or new love.
Discover your own inspired success strategy.
You've already experienced grace in your
lifetime. Why not acknowledge and follow
your own Yellow Brick Road?

*Today, I reflect on how I have succeeded
before. I acknowledge and uncover my
own Yellow Brick Road.*

20 *october*

· · · · · · · · · · · · · · ·

In transition? Remember, an architect doesn't
attach the expensive Spanish windows or
frame the structure of the castle until the
foundation is secure. You are establishing a
foundation, scraping through dirt, and laying
concrete. And if it's taking time, it's because
you keep questioning the foreman and
holding up the shovels.

*Today, I stop questioning the timing
of things.*

21 *october*

. . . .

Today, I breathe out everything I think
I should be. I breathe in everything I am
meant to be. I let go of false, invalidating
conditioning. I breathe in the certain. My
real power comes when I am my real self.

*Today, I breathe out everything I think
I should be. I breathe in everything
I am.*

22 *october*

. . . .

Sometimes life might feel so complicated, like
a drain clogged with the hair of Rapunzel.
Or a mob of decisions battering your brain
like a tornado whipping debris. But do not
lose sight of the power and privilege you
possess this day. You are alive. You are in the
game of games. You have this time. There
will be a day when you'd give anything for
a moment like this.

Today, I know I am in the game
of games. I am alive and I have
opportunities.

. . . .

My vulnerability is my strength. When I feel
fragile, I reach out to the Mystery for comfort
and direction. I am answered with silken,
expansive blessings. I am met with intimacy
and shifts and songs on the radio just for me.
I am grateful for whatever it takes for me to
have this astonishing experience.

*Today, I am grateful that my
vulnerability connects me to
my ultimate strength.*

. . . .

Rip up your scorecard, baby. Sit at the doorstep of Magical Possibility. Step into this uncorrupted moment and allow your years, disappointments, and opinions to disappear. Call it Zen. Amnesia. Surrender. The Zone. Whatever lingo works for you. Because as a career and an inspired success coach, I know this breakthrough strategy works: *Be willing to allow things to work out, even if they haven't worked out before.*

Today, I have the willingness to allow things to work out, even if they haven't worked out before.

25 *october*

. . . .

Comparison is such a fun-house mirror.
You look at what you think someone else has.
Then you look at what you think you don't
have. I keep learning that the part of me
who is "doing the looking" is the one who
is already pained and insecure. I have to
ignore what she's looking at and look at her
with great love instead.

Today, I remember that it's not what
I see that upsets me.

26 *october*

. . . .

The "middle moments" are our ashrams,
boot camps, graduate schools, and launch
pads. They are anything but useless, empty,
or ordinary. The middle of things is where
change takes place, where the great big barge
of how things have always been turns around
in the ocean and goes a new way. Sometimes
it feels slower than a long red light, but real
change changes your whole life.

Today, I know that when I'm in the
middle of things, I'm changing
everything.

· · · · · · · · · · · · ·

We believe that if we could secure the right conditions or choose the exact right steps like some perfect fox-trot, *then* we would experience endless daisies on the hill, a happiness as good as cheesecake without calories, or pick your shade of Nirvana. But we are pursuing that which could never ever give us pleasure. Real freedom comes from the right use of the mind. (From *A Course in Miracles for Life Ninjas*)

Today, I'm not looking for the right conditions. I'm choosing the right use of my mind.

28 *october*

· · · · · · · · · · · · · · · · ·

Sometimes it will free you to let go of certain financial obligations or extravagant lifestyle choices. A life of spirit and substance will always outstrip a life of "style." You lust for excess only because you have deprived yourself of marrow.

Today, I am willing to free myself of extravagant financial obligations or the hunger for "more."

29 *october*

. . . .

The path of daring your true life can be as
terrifying as coming upon a mountain lion.
Yet it's also as breathtaking as coming out of
darkness and seeing a thousand buttercups in
golden light, or for some of us, a Starbucks
up ahead. Listening to your truth is an
adventure. And in the moments when
everything clicks into place, everything is
worth it. It's supposed to be this startling.
That's how you know you're alive.

*Today, I am willing to face my fears as
I choose the adventure of my true life.*

30 *october*

· · · · · · · · · · · · · · · ·

You can line your ducks up in a row. Or you
can spread your eagle wings and soar. Stop
trying to do everything "right." Listen to
what's right for you. Observe the holy and
compelling. Follow sideways magic.
An unlimited life doesn't come from a
prescription. It comes from revelation.

Today, I follow sideways magic.
I follow what compels me.

31 *october*

. . . .

You can't plan an inspired life. You can't see how things will fall together. I have seen clients stumble into the most serendipitous circumstances. If it had been a movie, it would have been contrived. There is some kind of plan or thread in each of us that has a deep gravitational pull. It's undeniable and infallible. Stop trying to figure it out. Let it out. There is more at work here than your limited understanding.

Today, I will trust each inspired moment to lead to the next one.

01 *november*

· · · · · · · · · · · · · · · ·

I read recently that snowflakes are all
alike. However, when they fall through the
atmosphere and interact with the elements,
they crystallize into their own unique
patterns. The way you fall in this life, the way
you meet the elements, this is your love song
to the Universe. The journey is what makes
you who you are.

*Today, I know that how I respond to my
trials creates who I am.*

02 *november*

. . . .

When I feel broken, I will sit down with
myself, put a silky arm around my bony
shoulders, sit and pray and be. I will not
smack this self across the face by wishing for
a different moment. I will not cut and paste
her reality. I will not push her aside, anxious
to move on. I will sit with this self, and her
difficulty, anxiety, or pressing lack of
certainty. I will sit with this self and be her
friend. I will sit there until the sun goes down
and rises and burns itself out. I will never
leave. I will never ask for more or better.

*Today, I will be there for myself even
in difficult times.*

· · · · · · · · · · · · · ·

Don't join that dismal bandwagon of thieves
who believe that it's more successful to just
tack things together than to be naked on the
path of pursuing your truth. Do not borrow
knowledge from the ones who do not dare.
The ones who dare absolutely know the pain
of being in the middle of things. If your life is
unsettled, imperfect, unpredictable, wild at
the core, stuck, or yet to "come together,"
congratulations. You're in the stream of
being wholly alive.

*Today, I honor myself for daring to
be wholly in the middle of things.*

04 *november*

. . . .

When you want only love, you will see
nothing else. We are training ourselves to
look for love. We are training ourselves to
look for what's going right. We are training
ourselves to behold the spirit in others and
in ourselves. You can't hold on to a limited
vision of someone else and have an unlimited
vision of yourself. (From *A Course in Miracles
for Life Ninjas*)

*Today, I behold the spirit in everyone
and my possibilities expand.*

05 *november*

. . . .

You don't know which circumstance is the
big one and which one is small. You don't
have the tools with which to measure the
creativity of a Presence that shatters and
cultivates your understanding at the same
time. This chef runs a completely different
kind of kitchen. Nothing follows precedent,
though nothing is by accident. (From *Inspired &*
Unstoppable: Wildly Succeeding in Your Life's
Work!)

Today, I will not decide that this
circumstance is a big one or a
small one.

06 *november*

. . . .

I'm not advocating struggle for struggle's sake, but I am honoring the kind of struggle that gives way to conviction. The inner struggle defines your wingspan. You just can't know the breadth of flight without a certain kind of fight. You can't experience the glory hallelujah of the other side until you've almost died. (From *This Time I Dance! Creating the Work You Love*)

Today, I honor the places where I struggle. I am moving toward conviction.

· · · · · · · · · · · · · · · ·

Those of us who dare to live a larger life
often feel smaller and more uncertain. We are
walking naked into the unknown. We are
leaving behind the safety of mass agreement
and approval. It would be a sad situation
if we truly were alone. But we're not. We
have *guidance*. We have a knowing sense
within us, a meaningful compass, a tender
companion with no shortage of good advice
and rocket fuel. This Beloved One will
empower us beyond any kind of security we
ever knew before. We need to feel uncertain
so that we call upon this certainty.

*Today, I use my uncertainty to call
upon the Certainty of the Beloved.*

08 *november*

· · · · · · · · · · · · · · · ·

When I face my fears, I make exquisite deals
with myself. I whisper to myself, "Honey, you
can back out if you need, no questions
asked." I encourage myself to try. And I offer
compassion for myself all along the way.
Because I give myself permission to take a
step backward when I need it, I'm willing to
take a step forward. And with each step
forward, I'm in, and the flow of moving in the
right direction can buoy me.

*Today, I give myself permission to step
forward and to back out if I need it.*

. . . .

We're not here to prove anything. We're not here to force growth or commitment. We're here to stay honest about what is possible in any given moment. It's an experiment. It's an expedition. It's the expansion of identity. It's the willingness to walk outside of your comfort zone and see what it's really like. Are you willing to let yourself experience something true, rather than assume you know what it will be like?

Today, I am willing to walk past my assumptions and experiment.

10 *november*

. . . .

I want you to stay with the activity your True
Self wants you to do. Stay a little longer. Go
beyond, even a wisp, where you have gone
before. Walk past the demon of knee-jerk
reaction. Stay present. You can discover an
untapped well, a spring of shocking love,
your inner Atman or Goddess. Ask yourself:
*Will it hurt more to stay with this—or will it
hurt more to not stay with this?* Slow down,
breathe, and make a conscious choice.

*Today, I stay present and longer with
something my True Self wants me to do.*

11 *november*

. . . .

Let timing defer to truth, not truth to timing.
Dare to take the time it takes. Dare to follow
the crazy path of birthing genius. Support
your creative, organic, uncanny process. Do
not wrestle it to the ground and tie it to a slide
rule. Remember, you are co-creating with
mysterious powers that work on multiple
levels all at the same time. Drop the clock and
buckle up. Work big and work true. It's not
that important to get something done. It's
important to let your limits be undone. (From
*Inspired & Unstoppable: Wildly Succeeding in
Your Life's Work!*)

*Today, I let things take the time
they take.*

12 *november*

· · · · · · · · · · · · · · · ·

Guidance is like candlelight. It lights up a
room or a moment in time. I can see where
I am right now. I can't see where I'm going.
But I bring this flicker with me as I step
forward. (From *This Time I Dance!
Creating the Work You Love*)

*Today, I step forward without knowing
where I'm going. Guidance will arrive
in each step.*

13 *november*

. . . .

The life you imagine is real. Even if you're
in a dull job and your boss just yelled at you,
you're still a Broadway performer. You're still
the CEO of a nutrition empire, the beloved
partner of your right mate, or whatever your
calling is. Your identity doesn't change. Your
circumstances may not match you yet. But
your essence is more real than your
circumstance.

*Today, I believe in what is true about
me, even if it's not here yet.*

14 *november*

. . . .

Are you setting goals that fit into your life? If they're real goals, they will blow up your life, drag you out to sea, push your head under water, and make you gasp for air—and see the light. Real goals are an identity shift.

Today, I set a goal that frightens me.

15 *november*

. . . .

There's a wild-shouting, joyful plan for my
life and I'm going to say yes to my nature, yes
to my desires, yes to my heart's thundering
power and maverick freedom. It makes no
sense to try to be what I am not. What I am
IS the plan.

*Today, I will not fight myself. What
I am IS the plan.*

16 *november*

. . . .

Many of us ask for "guidance" or "direction,"
but then shove the answer back, or try to
rough up the messenger in hopes of maybe
dislodging another seemingly more practical
message. We want the voice of inspiration to
sound like something reasonable, familiar,
preferably brimming with action items and
Venn diagrams, kind of like a project
manager in a suit. We're not really listening
as much as listening for only what we think
we want to hear.

Today, I am willing to listen to
anything my guidance has to say,
not just what I want to hear.

17 *november*

· · · · · · · · · · · · · · ·

Opportunities do not come to fill a lack.
They come as an expression of a fullness
you already have. How can you feel more full
right now? What activities or relationships
raise your energy or make you feel as though
you have more to give? If you want to attract
opportunities to you, use the ones you have.

Today, I focus on filling myself up.
I have the opportunity to . . .

18 *november*

· · · · · · · · · · · · · · · ·

There is a jaguar within you, unafraid in
every way. There is an endless parade of
creativity, delight, and surprise marching
through your heart. You are so much more
than you know. Keep saying yes to what your
instincts desire. When you honor your true
nature, you discover a constellation of other
powers.

*Today, I say yes to my desire and
strength.*

19 *november*

. . . .

I found that not rushing, and giving my project my full attention, flung open the floodgates. I won the lottery of the mind. I could lose and find myself in the same place. And here's the day when everything changes. It's the day we realize that we're not doing our work to *get* somewhere as much as to *be* somewhere right now. We're no longer desperate to land. We're just crazy for the magic carpet ride.

Today, I attend to my life and work in order to be *here, rather than try to "get there."*

. . . .

I couldn't imagine how my "baby steps"
would take me anywhere significant. Now
I know that there's no such thing as baby
steps. Every step is courageous and heroic
and ushers you into unimaginable growth.
Every step you take to support your talent or
gift activates a divine serum within you and
a stream of good coming your way. (From
*Inspired & Unstoppable: Wildly Succeeding in
Your Life's Work!*)

*Today, I take a "baby step" toward my
right life.*

21 *november*

. . . .

Praise and money may pay your bills, but not
your rent here on earth. The landlord wants
more from you and you know it. Really, you
will evict yourself if you deny yourself for
too long. You simply cannot just keep going
through the motions when the wildness is
within you. It costs too much to live without
living. You can suffocate or disappear in
broad daylight.

*Today, I will not just go through the
motions. I invite wildness.*

22 *november*

. . . .

Give yourself permission to be gentle with
yourself today. You are carrying many
loads—responsibilities, dreams, and
uncertainties. Gentleness is not weakness.
It is a kindness that allows the soul to breathe
and supply natural strength and direction.
Only self-cruelty is weakness.

Today, I will be gentle with myself.

23 *november*

. . . .

You may doubt yourself, but you cannot
change the nature of your reality. You are
infinitely loved, guided, and protected, even
when you've yelled at your cat, drank too
much wine, or secretly didn't donate to a very
good cause. Your Spirit will never let you fall.
You may falter, but you cannot change the
substance of your being. You are perfect love,
seeking to express itself.

Today, I know that nothing can change
the perfect love of Spirit within me.

24 *november*

. . . .

Sometimes you will follow your soul
and others will feel alienated from you.
Sometimes you will follow your soul and
others will feel connected to you. But you
can feel connected to others only when
you follow your soul.

Today, I seek only the connection.

25 *november*

. . . .

Gratitude ends fear. Count your blessings,
sweet royal fool. The Universe has so much
more to give you. You were never meant to
focus on what you didn't get. You were meant
to focus on all that you have been given, for
this is the love that was sent to you for a
reason.

*Today, I will recount over and over all
that I've been given.*

26 *november*

· · · · · · · · · · · · · · · · ·

Refuse to be conditioned. Stay innocent.
Remember, you have never been down this
road before. There is no road, baby. There is
only desire or desire repressed. There is only
being present or projecting from an unhealed
past. There is only mad magic. Or mad magic
conspiring to be revealed.

Today, I open up to a road I've never
been on before.

27 *november*

. . . .

We, who are questioning our lives and our
abilities, are the light of the world. We will be
a beacon of comfort, hope, and direction to
those who need us. We are in the soup, but
it is healing broth. We are the ones who are
learning to find freedom in the midst of
bruised conditions. Every spiritual tradition
teaches us that freedom is not being liberated
once the job comes through, the check comes
in, or the skinny jeans fit. Freedom is
learning how to be at peace no matter what,
no matter when.

*Today, I know that my struggles can
provide comfort and direction for
others at a later time.*

28 *november*

. . . .

You may be one of the ones who know that
your circumstances are not your identity.
You may know that the reality on the tongues
of others is not the reality of your insistent
heart. You are awake. Do not duck when you
were born to stand proud. Do not conform
when it is your calling to inform. You are here
to ignite the lives of others, not copy them.

*Today, I am willing to remain awake
and ignite the lives of others.*

29 *november*

. . . .

When we face challenges and losses in our
lives, we often can't see how a Higher Love
would allow this to happen. We turn our lack
of understanding into a loss of trust. We draw
a line in the sand and give up. We think we
are protecting ourselves from getting hurt.
But we are endangering ourselves. We are
shutting down to what we really want,
hardening ourselves by rejecting every
possibility except an embittered one. The
sun is still shining. But sunlight cannot get
through brick.

Today, I ask a Higher Love to help me
trust in Higher Love.

30 *november*

· · · · · · · · · · · · · · · · ·

Decide that all is well. Only you can decide
to bless your life. It is not a matter of faith
from the deities, the right breeze, or three
cherries in a row. It won't be any different
when you get the white Mercedes or an
adoring spouse. Your mind will choose new
goals, carrots, obsessions, and bargaining
chips. Make the decision to celebrate your
life now. You've been waiting for your own
blessing all along.

*Today, I remember that I am only
waiting for my own blessing.*

01 *december*

. . . .

Sometimes as we open up to our creativity,
we dilute our self-expression because we
want to fit in. But I tell my clients to follow
exultation instead of expectation. Dare to
ditch labels or marketable tracks. Resist the
urge to wedge yourself into a category.
Instead, answer a hunger, name a storm, and
find your own way to oxygen. You were born
to answer a question and to be that answer.

*Today, I know that I was born to
answer a question and to be that
answer.*

02 *december*

. . . .

It's a blessing to have a strong intellect.
Yet use your intellect to serve your heart,
not to fight it. In the hands of a builder, a
turbo chainsaw can create order, grace, and
a place to live. The heart is that builder. The
mind, that powerful tool. Some of the great
work of this life will be learning how to use
all of your faculties. Please do not fight
yourself, but fight for yourself.

*Today, I use the powers of my mind to
serve the powers of my heart.*

03 *december*

. . . .

A lack of patience is a form of self-hatred with
beady little eyes. It's a form of self-attack. It's
a barrier between where you are right now
and everything you want. As you connect to
yourself, you discover your foundation and
freedom. You won't need to get somewhere
else. You won't need to be someone else. You
will never find your potential in the future.

Today, I have patience with myself.

. . . .

Being overwhelmed does not come from
too much to do. It comes from lack of clarity.
When you're clear, you know you don't need
to do everything. You just have to do the right
thing. The right thing is always the one step
you feel guided to do right now.

*Today, I remind myself that I don't need
to do everything. I need to do the right
thing.*

05 *december*

. . . .

It is not a crime to feel sad. It is not "lower
thinking." Creating a meaningful life means
allowing yourself to cradle every aspect of the
spectrum of life, not just the ones you deem
"right." Love is the fabric within all of it.
If you do not judge or resist your experience,
you will enter it with freedom and it will offer
you freedom and release.

Today, I do not need to "be positive."
I show up for all of my feelings with
awareness and love.

. . . .

Remember, there is an Inspired Power within you that can and will support you in anything. You are worth this lifetime. You are worth more love than you know. You are worthy of miracles. Do not assume that something you desire is impossible. Instead, walk in this exact direction. It is in the realm of the "impossible" that you discover how loved you are.

Today, I know that there is an Inspired Power within me that can engineer "impossible" results.

07 *december*

. . . .

I have arrived and I'm arriving still. It's an ongoing state of development. I'll always be hungering for more because I'll always have new things to express. But I choose now to see my hunger as the precursor of my realization—not as a lack of accomplishment. If I'm creatively alive, it's always going to be a mixed bag of arriving and still having further to go. (From *Inspired & Unstoppable: Wildly Succeeding in Your Life's Work!*)

Today, I recognize that I will always be arriving and having further to go.

08 *december*

. . . .

If you're wondering if you could ever make it
in the wide world without a plan or a clue,
an eye of newt or a sinew of an idea, you can.
The ball of yarn is in you—it will unravel. It
will thread itself into garments and destinies.
It will lay down a path before you of bright
warmth to be followed and it will never run
out. It will weave a destiny for you if you
grant it safe passage. It will take you all the
way, when you follow your own true way.

*Today, I will go all the way by following
the thread of my own true way.*

. . . .

You do not want more control over your life.
You want more trust. You want to know
that things are moving quietly, effortlessly,
and favorably in your direction. You do not
want to push all the buttons, supervise,
calibrate, double-check, and hammer down
every detail. You want to be lifted into a life
more arresting and harmonious than any you
could manufacture.

*Today, I am focusing on trusting more
than on seeking control.*

10 *december*

. . . .

The "tough times" bring us to our depths.
The depths bring us to our heights. It's a
continuous spiral staircase. Whatever
troubles you right now will bring you to new
resourcefulness. Pain asks some crazy, soul-
scraping question for which you already
have the answer.

*Today, I know that through my pain,
I develop new resources.*

11 *december*

. . . .

Sometimes you are stuck because you're
trying to heal your marriage all at once,
launch your business in an hour, or scale a
mountain in one foothold. Break your big,
bold, life-changing desire into a thousand
flea-size baby steps. It's easy to move forward
when it's simple to move forward.

*Today, I break down my desire into a
thousand tiny steps.*

12 *december*

· · · · · · · · · · · · · · · ·

Times of change push us to realize that we have reservoirs of strength and spiritual acuity we have not yet uncovered. Most of us scuffle for the comfort of the known, rather than salute the blue dragon of the unknown. The True Self emerges as a response to pain. Without familiar crutches, we discover wings. Change isn't happening to us. *It's happening for us.* It's pressing us to use our attributes.

Today, I know that change is happening for *me.*

13 *december*

· · · · · · · · · · · · · ·

You may live and consume in a more unpretentious fashion in order to support the life you truly desire. You may stray from the "American Dream" in order to follow your own. It takes courage to articulate and live your values. But remember, it's never a step down to step ahead in your life. Take back your freedom. Put your money where your meaning is.

Today, I spend my money consciously on products and services that feed my sense of meaning.

14 *december*

. . . .

My family wanted me to have a secure job, a
big beige house with a thick green lawn. But
I ached to touch the skies. I couldn't find
security in stifling my love. I couldn't rest in
what gave others rest. The only security
I have found has come from listening to the
call to be myself. There is so much more ease
in following your truth than in denying it.

Today, I honor what gives me a sense of
security rather than what others tell me
is security.

15 *december*

. . . .

Chinese bamboo grows in a way that looks
as though nothing is happening. The roots
are growing furiously deep. Suddenly the
stalks can shoot up eighty feet in six weeks.
Transition is like that, too. First you do your
root work. Then all heaven breaks loose.

*Today, I remember that when it seems
like "nothing is happening," my roots
are growing furiously deep.*

16 *december*

. . . .

Become a witness of your own success—if
you want to have any, that is. Celebrate being
in the middle of things, on your way, and
having arrived in so many ways. Practice
basking in what you have and who you are. If
you continue to take your success for granted,
nothing will change for you, even if everything
changes. (From *Inspired & Unstoppable:
Wildly Succeeding in Your Life's Work!*)

*Today, I bask in all the ways I've
already arrived in my life.*

17 *december*

. . . .

Fear is a call to love ourselves more. I tell
myself: "I will walk with you through
anything. I will not judge you. I know you are
doing the best you can. You are surrounded
by power-angels, enveloped by grace, and
will always know what to do. Breathe."

*Today, I will walk with myself through
anything.*

18 *december*

. . . .

The best way to get out of fear is to just not get into it. Become a self-love ninja. Earn your black belt in the art of self-encouragement. Take self-criticism out of your diet. Stop being petty; you can't afford it. Focus on *any* movement in the right direction. This fuels hope, accomplishment, stamina, and momentum. It's harder to get into a negative groove when you're on a positive roll.

Today, I will become a self-love ninja.

19 *december*

· · · · · · · · · · · · · · · ·

A mechanical life requires output, form, and
results measured down to the chin hair of the
decimal point. An organic life is natural. It's
blemished and mythic. You will not endlessly
"produce" without having the times of
contraction to get to know yourself again and
again—and summon your riotous forces.

Today, I am willing to be "unproductive"
by my ego's standards of productivity.

20 *december*

. . . .

Ditch the stoic, the intellectual, and Ms. Rosy
Pants. Sometimes you need to hoot your joy.
And sometimes you need to cry or kick
something. Can you allow yourself to simply
feel how you feel at this moment in your life?
Let your emotions or inner child "speak"
to your Wise Self. Share your feelings with
your therapist, coach, shaman, or favorite
raccoon—anyone who will not seek to change
you. Honesty is a healer. A feeling is a feeling.
It is not reality.

Today, I feel my feelings with self-
honesty. They are just feelings.

21 *december*

. . . .

Your pain is your insistent guru. How do
you glean instruction from the sting? How
do you resist the urge to curse it, deny it, or
lie down in a ball for a thousand years? How
do you love yourself? How do you forgive
yourself? How do you sit down right now and
trust the perfection of where you are? This is
the juncture of your freedom. It's not about
sweeping the kitchen or sending in a résumé.
True accomplishment is about feeding the
wild bluebird in your heart berries not of
this world.

*Today, I trust that my pain has
something to teach me.*

22 *december*

. . . .

I am ripening into my full promise now.
That means I am shedding old skins,
dropping personas and roles. I will not be
who others expect me to be. I will say no. I
will give myself more time. I have a sacred
responsibility to my light. I am willing to
disappoint others, but I am not willing to
disappoint myself anymore. I am a servant
to the bold appointment within me.

*Today, I am willing to drop a role or
persona. I am willing to disappoint
someone else rather than myself.*

23 *december*

The mountain that obstructs a caterpillar
daunts not his winged incarnation. The
possibilities change as we do. That's why
your dilemma doesn't matter. It's a problem
of perspective. A caterpillar will never figure
out or handle a butterfly's path. But you will.
You are in the transformation now. (From
*This Time I Dance! Creating the Work
You Love*)

*Today, I don't need to figure out how
to get past obstacles.*

24 *december*

. . . .

The Universe isn't like a rotten boyfriend
who loses interest in you if, say, you gain
some extra pounds or chins. Spirit never
forgets your birthday or any day in which you
exist. The love of the Universe is not fickle,
narcissistic, or dependent on you counting
the exact right number of mala beads. *Sacred
love is consistent.*

*Today, I rest in the love of the Universe
that has consistently been here for me.*

25 *december*

. . . .

You have a winning hand, before you even
pick up your cards. You have nothing but
aces and kings. Or a royal flush. You were
born golden. You were born beautiful. You
have everything you need. It doesn't matter
who raised you, who left you, who fired you,
how old you are, or if you have cancer, you're
deaf, broke, disabled, or dying. You are free.
You have a Higher Self that can do anything.
(From *A Course in Miracles for Life Ninjas*)

Today, I know I have a Higher Self
that can do anything.

. . . .

Please don't let anyone else's lack of love change how loving you can be. Be the one who loves, even if others don't know how. Be the one who loves, even when others complain, eat the last of your favorite cookies, or vote for candidates who you know are less intelligent than your average housefly. Be the one who listens and doesn't try to change someone. Be the one who is kind, even when others are gruff with pain. The more loving you are, without expectation, the better you will feel. Of course, be loving to yourself first.

Today, I will not allow someone else's lack of love change how loving I can be.

27 *december*

. . . .

Great Love knows me better than I know myself. I know only my current self. But my soul knows all my capacities, my destiny, and the spectrum of my life's potential. I don't always get "my way," which is a blessing. Because I continue to grow. And as I do, my desires continue to grow, too. I used to only want a life that helped me stay safe. Now I want a life that helps me fly. I no longer want a bunker. I want a ride.

Today, I acknowledge that I don't always know my own highest good.

28 *december*

. . . .

Sacred love is consistent. Think of a time
when things worked out for you. The same
loving, guiding intelligence is with you now.
No matter what's going on, you are still safe.
You're on the bus, headed in the best
direction. The scenery outside the window
may change, but the bus driver hasn't
changed a smidgeon. Love is at the wheel.

*Today, I know that no matter what
happens, Love is at the wheel.*

29 *december*

. . . .

As a new year approaches, you may be
deciding on your goals, aspirations, or
focus. Can you be intentional, but not
aggressive? Can you allow your spirit instead
of your brain to choose your goals? Your
new year already has a life of its own.
Something wants to be born. It's the right
time. Don't miss the cues because you
"have a plan."

*Today, as I consider my intentions for
the new year, I know something already
wants to be born.*

30 *december*

. . . .

You are nearing the threshold of another year.
It's time to bless the year you've lived, no
matter what. There was not one random
moment this year. Every occurrence gave
you tremendous gifts. It changed you in
some way. The new year will depend on
how you see this past year. What happened
for you in these last twelve months that
will propel you in a truer direction?

*Today, I am grateful for the occurrences
this past year that give birth to my true
direction in the new year.*

31 *december*

Today is the last day of this year of your life.
This year will never come again. Bow as this
teacher exits. It has laced your challenges
with soul gifts. Set you up for true joy.
Brought you to new vows. The more you find
gratitude for the year that has been, the more
you will delight in the one that arrives.

Today, I honor all this year has been
for me.

A Final Word:
Let's Stay in Touch and Inspired

I am so honored to have shared some or all of this year with you. I'd love to tell you a bit about my vision for all of us living in magnificence.

I want to live in a world of awakened capacities. I want you to join me in creating this world where more of us live fearless, inspired lives. We have our dreams for a reason.

I'd love for us to stay inspired together.

Many of us are bridge people: We are left-brained and right-brained. We are analytical and creative. We are sensitive and grounded. We are drawn to the light and yet have our feet on the ground. We are here to create our dreams and the dreams the world needs us to bring forth. We are learning to maximize our potential and the potential of humanity.

We are stepping into new territories.

We may even lend the disciplines of creativity and spirituality, authority in a world that has often minimized these non-linear powers.

We are here to create a culture of undoing fear and opening to endless resources. In our own lives, we are choosing love instead of fear—daily. We are training our minds and hearts to soar. Please join me.

I would love to continue supporting you in this life practice, and on this amazing journey.

Please visit me at **TamaKieves.com/free365** and sign up to get a FREE week of A Year Without Fear, a subscription-based service to help inspire you *daily* with guided five-minute *audio* mind-set shifts. I'll read you the mind-set shift for the day and then lead you in a guided meditation. I want my voice to speak to your inner voice. I want to empower and inspire your mind-set for five minutes of your day.

Or just stop by the website, as it's the mainline of continuous support. Pick up my free e-newsletter and say hello and tell me about your experience with this material. Please do join me in your city for a workshop or retreat. Or invite me to speak to your organization, collaborate with your institute, or offer a retreat at your villa. Just saying. Really, I LOVE hearing from you.

And do get connected to my/your awesome tribe of like-minded individuals through social media. I post daily on Facebook.com/TamaKieves and on Twitter @TamaKieves, LinkedIn, and by carrier pigeon, if you prefer.

And just so you have all my channels of communication: You can reach me through Tama Kieves International, at www.TamaKieves.com or PO Box 9040, Denver, CO 80209. Or call 1-800-334-8114.

I wish you years without fear.

A Year's Worth of Creative Inspiration

The Artist's Way Every Day
By Julia Cameron
ISBN: 978-1-58542-747-5

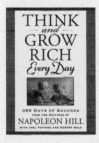

Think and Grow Rich Every Day
By Napoleon Hill with Joel
Fotinos and August Gold
ISBN: 978-1-58542-811-3

The Tao of Joy Every Day
By Derek Lin
ISBN: 978-1-58542-918-9

More Wisdom to Create a Life You Love,
from Tama Kieves

This Time I Dance!:
Creating the Work You Love
ISBN: 978-1-58542-527-3

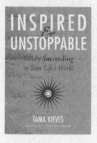

Inspired & Unstoppable: Wildly
Succeeding in Your Life's Work!
ISBN: 978-1-58542-929-5
(hardcover)
ISBN: 978-0-399-16578-8
(paperback)

If you enjoyed this book, visit

www.tarcherbooks.com

and sign up for Tarcher's e-newsletter to receive
special offers, giveaway promotions, and
information on hot upcoming releases.

TARCHER
PENGUIN

Great Lives Begin with Great Ideas

Connect with the Tarcher Community

• • •

Stay in touch with favorite authors!
Enter weekly contests!
Read exclusive excerpts!
Voice your opinions!

Follow us

 Tarcher Books

 @TarcherBooks

If you would like to place a bulk order
of this book, call 1-800-847-5515.